The Happy Professor

The Happy Professor

How to Teach Undergraduates and Feel Good About It

Bill Coplin

ROWMAN & LITTLEFIELD
Lanham • Boulder • New York • London

Published by Rowman & Littlefield
An imprint of The Rowman & Littlefield Publishing Group, Inc.
4501 Forbes Boulevard, Suite 200, Lanham, Maryland 20706
www.rowman.com

6 Tinworth Street, London SE11 5AL

Copyright © 2019 by Bill Coplin

All rights reserved. No part of this book may be reproduced in any form or by any electronic or mechanical means, including information storage and retrieval systems, without written permission from the publisher, except by a reviewer who may quote passages in a review.

British Library Cataloguing in Publication Information Available

Library of Congress Cataloging-in-Publication Data

Names: Coplin, William D., author.
Title: The happy professor : how to teach undergraduates and feel good about it / Bill Coplin.
Description: Lanham : Rowman & Littlefield, [2019] | Includes bibliographical references.
Identifiers: LCCN 2019003223 (print) | LCCN 2019010869 (ebook) | ISBN 9781475849073 (electronic) | ISBN 9781475849059 (cloth : alk. paper) | SBN 9781475849066 (pbk. : alk. paper)
Subjects: LCSH: College teaching—United States—Handbooks, manuals, etc. | College teachers—United States—Handbooks, manuals, etc. | Teacher-student relationships—Handbooks, manuals, etc.
Classification: LCC LB2331 (ebook) | LCC LB2331 .C648 2019 (print) | DDC 378.1/25—dc23
LC record available at https://lccn.loc.gov/2019003223

Contents

Foreword	vii
Acknowledgments	ix
Introduction	xi
Part I: Roles	**1**
1 You	3
2 Artist	7
3 Skills Coach	11
4 Advisor	17
5 Boss	27
Part II: Strategies	**31**
6 Andragogy, Not Pedagogy	33
7 The Five Laws of the Minimalist	35
8 Everything Is Experiential	43
9 Evaluate Yourself	47
Part III: Engagement Tactics	**51**
10 Use Undergraduate Teaching Assistants	53
11 Use Dale Carnegie Speeches	57
12 Create Groups for Small In-Class Assignments	59
13 Set the Stage in the First Class	61
14 Use Simulations and Role Plays	63

15	Lie to the Class	65
16	Keep Your Mouth Shut	67
17	Make Laptops and Smartphones Helpful	69

Part IV: Organizational Tactics — 71

18	Start with the Concrete and Familiar	73
19	Use Modules	75
20	Use Class Time for Coaching	77
21	Debriefing Competitions	79
22	Create Lateness and Absence Policies	81
23	Distinguish Between Points Earned and Points Lost	83
24	Use Extra-Credit Points to Stimulate Extra Practice	85
25	Use Group Presentations as Teamwork Practice	87

Part V: Remedial Tactics — 89

26	Writing to Communicate	91
27	Improve Typing	93
28	Simple Computer Applications	95
29	Excel Is Life	97
30	Information Searching Basics	99
31	Survey Basics Required	101
32	Quantitative Tools Are Not About Mathematics	103

Part VI: Citizenship Tactics — 105

33	The Easy Way to Community Engagement	107
34	Use Continuums to Avoid the Role of Propagandist	109
35	Use Problem-Solving Exercises	113
36	The Order, Freedom, Equality Triangle	115
37	The Grading Exercise	119
38	The Prince System	123

Conclusion: Where Do You Go From Here? — 125

Appendix A: The Grading Exercise: Student Guide and Discussion Following the Exercise — 127

Appendix B: Directions for Forecasting with the Prince System — 131

About the Author — 137

Foreword

When I first became a dean in 1995, I was curious about how to find and hire transforming professors—the kind of inspiring, intense, caring, and demanding teachers who had made such a difference in my own education. In interviews at the beginning of their careers, these folks do not obviously stand out among their peers. Years and decades later it becomes obvious that they are wonderfully different.

Back in 1995, I collected hundreds of memoirs authored by these teachers and their students, trying to find and code the common attributes or predictors, so that if possible, I could hire more of them than other schools. It was a humbling experience. The most common attribute turned out to be a healthy disdain for administrators (like deans and chancellors).

Syracuse University has many of these transforming teachers, and the students revere them even while they confide that they are "hard." The author of this book is one of the most remarkable. Professor Bill Coplin directs the Public Affairs Program in the Maxwell School. His Public Affairs 101 course has enrolled more than 40,000 students so far. It is hard. Bill is demanding, even curmudgeonly. He insists students learn and manifest the skills of a competent professional while also coming to understand citizenship and what it concretely means to do good.

I have seen Bill teach. He knows his students. He demands a lot of them, but that is because he sees extraordinary promise that others may overlook. He relentlessly advocates for his students, including for jobs and careers. He on occasion (surprise) quietly manifests a healthy disdain for administrators. And he is a treasure to this university and our students.

This book captures the essence of Bill Coplin, a transforming teacher who has influenced thousands of lives. May it inspire and influence you in your own teaching, regardless of the format or methods by which you inspire the learners in your life.

Chancellor Kent Syverud
Syracuse University

Acknowledgments

This book has been in the writing since 2014 when my daughter suggested I write a memoir. When she found out it was not a personal memoir but a professional memoir, she dropped me like a hot potato but with much love. She got me started, so that is why she is in the acknowledgment.

I spent two years writing a memoir, but eventually gave that up because too many memoirs are written by academics and no one would buy that book. Help from colleagues who ran out of steam reading the memoir also convinced me that I was on the wrong path.

Then I realized, in talking with Chancellor Kent Syverud, who wrote the foreword to this book, and a very wise board of trustee member, Judy Seinfeld, that what I wanted was for more people to teach like me. I had been writing how-to books for some time, so of course I felt more comfortable. Judy gave me a pep talk as I give my students, which created the fear that the next time I saw her she would ask about the book.

I had no trouble writing this self-help book quickly using some things from the professional memoir and most things from my everyday experiences. I was fortunate to have a grant to cover the cost of hiring students to help me in the editorial process. Madeleine Buckley and then Jennifer Glass not only proofread but made suggestions. The most frequent one was "Stop ranting." There would be no book without them. Carly Powell provided proofreading assistance.

Publishers now want a social media presence, so Kate Alexis Ramos Abogado tried to teach me how to tweet, which is an ongoing project for her replacement, Neeve Prendergast. I mention them because the desire for a social media presence forced us to come up with and develop the brand Happy Professor. That brand drove a set of major revisions in the book.

I have had help from my professional colleagues whose full-time job is to teach and think about teaching. Martha Diede, who came to Syracuse in the fall of 2018 as director of the Center for Teaching and Learning Excellence, read the manuscript and made a series of clever suggestions. She shares many of my views but helped me most by bringing her extensive knowledge and experience in helping us all teach better. Austin Zwick, a newly hired teaching professor in my department, read the manuscript and made several useful suggestions, which I used in revising the book. Cherry McCabe, who teaches at Simpson University in northern California, has shown me many and better ways to use skills and experiences to create students who do well and do good.

Finally, I want to thank the staff of Rowman & Littlefield and particularly Sarah Jubar, who has done a wonderful job suggesting changes and copyediting the manuscript.

Introduction

Don't worry; be happy!

—Bobby McFerrin, songwriter

I am now 79 years old and have been teaching full time since 1964, first at Wayne State University and then at Syracuse University beginning in 1969. I continue to run an undergraduate program and teach three or four courses each semester, and I have no plans to retire. I plan to drop dead in my freshman course in our beautiful 200-seat auditorium. I am very lucky to have a job and a calling that gives me so much happiness.

How could I not be happy? I want to do good by giving students the tools they need to promote a better world, regardless of their ideology. I want to help students transform themselves from confused teens or adults into people with a clear path to do well and do good. I feel particularly happy when I am able to help students from a disadvantaged background find a path to their own social mobility. My life is full of young people who allow me to act like a child if I feel like it. I get my summers off, and I can make my own work schedule. I receive many privileges that I deeply appreciate. I can study society by observing my students as part of my work.

I still have to pay $1,200 for parking on campus, but I see it as my price of admission to my house of fun. Finally, I love my students and most of them love me. I have hundreds of thank-you notes from students to entertain me any time I feel like it.

One of the things that has disturbed me over the years is seeing that so many of my colleagues—both at Syracuse University and around the country—are unhappy. They complain about lack of student engagement, students being unprepared for college, and disagreements with colleagues or administrators over curriculum. They find tasks like grading papers burdensome.

They have some students they enjoy, but in many cases, they have too many students, which requires too many hours spent grading. If they are at a research institution, this means they have to write and publish, which takes them away from teaching.

They are also faced with a generation of students famous for their lack of attention, discipline, and seriousness about learning. However, today's students are not all that different from undergraduates since the beginning of time. Towns in the Middle Ages tried to stop colleges from setting up near them because students were such destructive and drunken knuckleheads.

If undergraduate professors approached teaching in the way that I suggest in this book, they would be much happier. Their lack of happiness is a result of the nature of undergraduate education today and the pressures coming from the institutions. The biggest historical factor is that undergraduate educational institutions have yet to adapt fully to the influx of students from all walks of life as a result of the GI Bill after World War II.

You cannot change the place of undergraduate education in society today, and you cannot change this institution that creates misery for so many undergraduate teachers. However, you *can* change yourself.

The secret to my happiness is that my primary educational goal is compatible with the goal of the students or parents and government who pay my salary. This goal can be simply stated: Prepare students to do well and do good in their careers and as citizens. Students want to be prepared for their life after college, and I want to help them.

Careers and citizenship are not the primary goal of unhappy teachers even though their institutions claim they are. They see their primary role as helping students learn the stuff they learn. The vast majority of students find that goal far-fetched, with little if any relationship to their own goals. Consequently, the majority of professors are frequently at odds with the vast majority of their students. This disconnect leads to apathetic, non-engaged, unhappy, and belligerent students.

This book is written for those unhappy college faculty and administrators, both in liberal arts and professional programs, working with either traditional or nontraditional students. It assumes that career preparation and effective citizenship must be the most important goals of undergraduate education. This does not mean these are your *only* goals, but they must be first.

You may wonder why you should take what I have to say seriously. My current chancellor, who has written the foreword to this book, provides his support for how I teach. Chancellor Syverud doesn't usually do this kind of thing, and for good reason. I am far from the mainstream of research university faculty. He must have meant it to take such a risk.

I also have more than 96 testimonials from alumni who feel that what they learned from my program has been important to their career success and their citizenship efforts. One such alum, Mark Hancock, wrote the following:

> The point of this is to thank the Public Affairs Program for the introduction your office made possible over 25 years ago. Without it, I might very well be back in Harpursville, NY painting houses to make ends meet while struggling to keep a farm operating. I have never forgotten how it changed my life, and I try to do my part to give back to the communities in which I live and work.

These anecdotal pieces of evidence, positive student evaluations, and my reviews on Rate My Professor may or may not convince you. I can't provide systematic empirical data on outcomes because it would be difficult to measure and demonstrate impact in terms of what students do. The only outcomes I can present are what students say and do while on campus and in their subsequent life.

Some of my supporters and non-supporters say my success is only because I am charismatic—a euphemism for "Panders to students." My colleagues may be right to some extent, but I have faith that the practices I follow play an important role in my students' successes.

There is no better test of the validity of the ideas in this book than for you to do your own research. Reading this book is not enough to test these ideas. The only way to test them is to try them yourself to see if they work for you as they did for me. Most likely, you will put your own spin on my ideas and experiences and discover what may or may not work for you.

The first section of this book describes the five roles of faculty teaching undergraduates, both in and out of the classroom.

The second section of the book is a list of five strategies that create an environment for students to help them develop the skills and perspectives they need to do well and do good. They are approaches that require students to learn by doing and to change their behavior as they prepare for careers and citizenship.

The last three sections of the book describe specific tactics I use in class and in interactions with students that motivate them to practice their skills and enhance their perspectives.

If you believe undergraduates should be treated more like children than adults, feel free to use this book as a sturdy door stop. If you are ready to at least entertain the idea that your job should be fun and not just building your students' knowledge base but helping them find viable career paths and become effective citizens, read on.

Part I

Roles

If you want to help students develop the skills and perspectives they need to do well and do good, you need to do more than teach courses and be a faculty advisor. This section suggests different ways to view and evaluate yourself as a professor. Think in terms of what you want to do to increase your happiness. Through these different roles, you are helping students prepare themselves for careers and citizenship as they learn the content you (and they) want them to learn. Remember that the students will be watching you as someone either to emulate or not to emulate. You should act as you want your students to act.

If you want to be a happy undergraduate professor, consider looking at the roles described in this section and helping students help themselves.

Chapter One

You

> There is only one happiness in this life, to love and be loved.
> —George Sand

You may think that as an undergraduate teacher, it should be all about the student. But before that, it has to be all about you. You may not like admitting that your self-interest is more important than your goals for your students, job, college, country, or the world. Yet to kid yourself into thinking otherwise could be the main obstacle to your happiness as an undergraduate professor. Every time you consider changing what you do as a professor, first ask, "What are the benefits and costs to me as a person?" You would not order a meal at a restaurant without asking yourself if your decision would make you happy, so why would you make a decision in your professional life without doing the same?

Most of the barriers to having fun as an undergraduate professor have to do with your own priorities. Here are some key guidelines.

1. The higher priority you give to undergraduate teaching, the happier you'll be.

Early on in my teaching career, I did many other things to either earn more money to support my family or to gain tenure and full professorship (which I luckily did by the age of 34). After the mid-1970s, my time and energy spent specifically teaching undergraduates increased, and so did my happiness.

2. The higher priority you give to helping students prepare for careers and citizenship while also covering basic content, the happier you'll be.

Since all disciplines present the scholarly material in the field, students are usually presented abstractions that are not easily related to things they know about. All undergraduate professors must have as their highest priority their students' careers and citizenship, which requires that the students see applications. This ultimately leads to an emphasis on skills as the centerpiece for all courses. The content is important for all professors but so are the skills. Skills, as a result, shape many of the roles, strategies, and tactics in this book.

3. The higher priority you give to treating students as young adults with differing needs, desires, and backgrounds, the happier you'll be.

Few professors would think students in a class of 30 are relatively homogenous in background and ability. Yet when they lecture and give multiple-choice tests, that is exactly what they are assuming. As you gain more experience, you realize that the first and most important principle of undergraduate teaching is to recognize the "individuality of the learner."

The "individuality of the learner" requires a social contract between the teacher and the student. It requires that professors recognize the legitimacy of the question "Why do I have to learn this?"

Ignoring or rejecting the individuality of the learner puts professors in a clear position of authority over the student, which leads to unhappy students. Students may feign respect for their professors' authority, but most do so only to get an A. Very few undergraduates want to learn what most professors want to impart, even though the professor deems it important. Most students do their coursework under what they see as the threat of low grades, no college degree, and a life of poverty. In reality, the majority of students want to learn what they find useful. Unhappy students produce unhappy professors.

The idea of the phrase "individuality of the learner" is similar in intent to Martin Luther's ideas of individuality of the priesthood. Luther wanted to reduce the barriers between the individual and God by constraining the role of the clergy. Similarly, you should reduce the barriers that prevent students from learning from you what will be useful to them and to society.

4. The higher priority you give to hands-on experiences in your courses, the more engaged and energetic your students will be and the more interested in their behavior you'll be.

Try including role-playing and simulation in your courses. Community service and internships also hold great potential to introduce students to content through experiences in and outside the university.

5. The higher priority you give to being efficient in preparing courses and dealing with students, the happier you'll be.

As the numbers of your students rise and your drive to give those students more opportunities that satisfy the individuality of the learner rise, your time and energy will also be taxed. That means you'll become less happy. However, you can develop strategies to reduce the time required to create new courses, improve existing ones, and have time for students. It's important to recognize your limitations and act to reduce the stress of overcommitment when helping undergraduates.

These are my personal guidelines. They are included here to suggest how you can weigh what you do in going about your business. It is all about priorities. To raise the priority for undergraduate teaching means lowering your priorities for other things. It means lowering your priority for research publications, unless you are able to get your students involved in the research process. It means reducing your service to your department and college by volunteering less and placing limits on engagement in planning and committees. It means spending less time with faculty colleagues and more time with your students.

These were the priorities that paved the road to my happiness. You may not select the exact same priorities or embrace them to the same extent. However, you must look at your priorities and decide how important being happy in teaching undergraduates is to you. My choices may be starker than yours would be. That is okay, but if you want to be happy, you must prioritize. Not all your goals can be a number-one priority.

As I tell my students, "Priorities are a bitch." The *B* word is used purposefully: to get their—and now your—attention. Being unclear about priorities is an occupational hazard for academics. It is part habit, part the fear of conflict, and part a conscious strategy, especially in meetings and decision-making forums. It is also a human instinct to avoid the uncertainty and stress that surround deciding and taking action. Priorities need to change as conditions change, but failing to realize the limit imposed by unclear and conflicting priorities can be a major source of unhappiness.

You might already know all of this. Unfortunately, knowledge does not lead to appropriate action. If you want to be a happy professor, you will need to think about your priorities and act on your thoughts. A student once asked a group of faculty, "Why do you spend so much time writing papers that only a handful of people will read when you could teach students what they will pass on to future generations?" We know where she is coming from. Where are you coming from?

Chapter Two

Artist

Art is not what you see, but what you make others see.

—Edgar Degas

In a letter to the Syracuse University community, Chancellor Syverud said that he could find no common denominator in the outstanding teachers he had studied except "a healthy disdain for administrators (like deans and chancellors)."

A healthy disdain toward authority lives in all artists, as well as all professors who act as artists. Artists communicate from their soul to those who see their work. While their efforts are driven by the need to express something for themselves, they want others to benefit in some way. For artists, it is personal.

Great teachers must be great artists. They must create experiences that provide a perspective that will capture the interest of and benefit the learner. Despite the pressures that come from their colleagues and accrediting agencies, teachers' efforts are what they want to teach, not what they are told to teach. This is particularly true in the humanities, social sciences, and professional schools.

Just as there is the individuality of the learner, there is also the individuality of the teacher. Just as the learner can be put in chains by the teacher and the system, teachers have to fight to break the chains that prevent them from creating a learning environment for their students. This threat to the individuality of the teacher is clearer at the K–12 level, where everyone seeks to control what goes on in the class. To a lesser extent, it is also present at the undergraduate level through outside pressures and demands for consensus among the various disciplinary and interdisciplinary tribes.

Fortunately, artists are in the business of breaking the chains of the past, and that is what you have to do. Now you may not see yourself as an artist, but you already are. You are the creator of an environment, one in which students either ignore you or change their behavior. Just as an artist hopes to move those observing his or her paintings to feel something, a teacher's goal is to engage, promote thought, and inspire something. That "something" may be a change in perspective or a decision to act.

Think of your teaching options as a painter's palette. It is the raw material from which you create a reality where students can learn from experience. Your teaching palette consists of lectures, readings, tests, assignments, and class discussions. It also has newer colors that have emerged over the past 50 years like simulations, role plays, internships, outside speakers, and student activities on campus. The most profound impact has been that of technology, especially the Web and social media. These tools include anything that may help students think and behave the way you want them to.

The idea that a teacher is an artist is particularly true if you accept the principle that the individuality of the learner requires students to connect to the experiences you provide. Teaching skills is about changing behavior, which requires an emotional attachment to the experiences you create. If your goal is to teach content and skills, you still need to be an artist. You need a deeper connection.

I came to this idea of approaching the task of teaching as an artist when developing my freshman course Introduction to the Analysis of Public Policy. The goal of this lower-division course is to provide students with the skills and perspectives to do well and to do good. I wanted to create an environment for the students to practice skills and to develop perspectives on societal problems and how government policies could ameliorate them.

My "paint" was in-class exercises that required many short, written assignments relating to entry-level public policy analysis. I put the paintbrush not in my hands but in their hands, having them practice writing and problem-solving skills.

Teachers, whether they know it or not, are creating an experience just like a playwright, a poet, or a painter. Even in a traditional curriculum, the readings they assign, the lectures they give, and the assignments they require are their creation. Sometimes they are not sure of their goals, but their success ultimately depends on whether or not they engage the students.

Just as artists differ, teachers differ. They create teachable moments when students are engaged and in a position to learn what is being taught. They create a dynamic landscape that students travel to develop their skills and their perspectives.

Seeing yourself as an artist will free you from internal constraints and relax you as you seek to embrace what you do as an act of creativity. It will be the closest thing you have experienced to the way it felt first falling in love with your subject matter during your undergraduate years, before you became constrained by the discipline and your professors. You will learn that whether or not your students "get it" or "don't get it" is a matter of the students' background, tastes, and capabilities. Their reactions, positive or negative, will force you to go back to the drawing board with a clear mission.

Chapter Three

Skills Coach

> I don't think I was a fine game coach . . . I think I was a good practice coach.
> —John Wooden, former UCLA head basketball coach

One of your most important roles in all your relationships with students is to coach them in developing a set of skills that they will need not only for their careers but also for citizenship and the rest of their lives. The author's book *10 Things Employers Want You to Learn from College* and his Skills Win website were created to anchor his efforts as a skills coach. His advising, conversations with students, and classes were all shaped by my goal to help students get the skills to do well and do good.

The book *10 Things Employers Want You to Learn from College* identified 38 skills divided into the 10 skill sets (see figure 3.1). Chapters were written for each of the 10 skill sets, telling students how they could develop skills both inside and outside class while they were in college.

Most faculty are already skills coaches to some extent, but the skills they support are needed in their research areas, especially for graduate students. An increasing number of undergraduate faculty have a broader set of skill goals, but they are not in the majority and rarely use the term "skills."

The number-one priority when making this list was that undergraduates must be able to understand the meaning of the listed skills. It is most important that the students understand the list because the skills are to become their educational goals. The faculty will need to understand that their technical terms don't work. These terms may offer more precision but not more clarity for the student.

A discussion of professors' use of terms is relevant to this point. A provost once suggested that the term "skills" should be replaced by the term "competencies" because the faculty would be turned off by the word "skills."

Students, however, would find the word "competencies" unfamiliar. This exchange illustrates why so many professors are unhappy and so many students tune out.

A, if not the, major component of undergraduate teaching is introducing students to words students never use. Most students never learn to speak or understand the language of the academic tribe unless they become members of the tribe. The faculty usually miss this point and conclude that the students are either stupid or not interested. How interested would you be in talking with someone who used words you didn't understand about a subject you needed to score an A in?

10 SKILL SETS

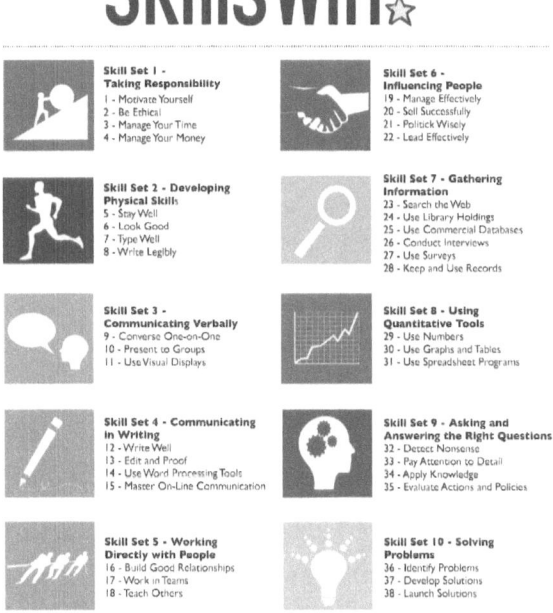

The skills to deal with the different backgrounds of people are essential—the skill sets of "Working Directly with People" and "Influencing People." As you look at the list of skills, you will see they are intentionally close to the language students use.

Others have suggested additional skills or revised terms, but the list is comprehensive enough. Some of these suggestions seem good, but the list was frozen back in 2003 and not subject to change. It is not because the list is perfect. It is because committees arguing over a list is a waste of time. A professor's time would be better spent being a skills coach rather than debating with colleagues over what the list should be. You can make up your own list. Just make sure the students can understand the terms.

Skills is a brand that encourages students to make skills acquisition their primary educational goal in college. A clear brand is the only way to get through the confusing, poorly defined, and frequently conflicting educational goals students are now given. The faculty, through their desire to expand their department's enrollment, bloat the curriculum and obscure the importance of skills. Take a look at the general education or liberal arts cores at most colleges, where there are hundreds or thousands of combinations of courses that satisfy the core. This bloat makes current curriculum look like congressional legislation, with a thousand pages for one law. No wonder students make high grades their number-one goal.

Replacing that goal with the goal of developing skills for a good career and good citizenship is much clearer and makes more sense to students. The bloat confuses students because what they have to learn never ends. The 10 skill sets, on the other hand, fit on one page. A list of skills in everyday language and, most importantly, as short as possible can bring some clarity and serve as a lighthouse for confused students.

Branding skills in the minds of students will allow them to decide if they buy the idea or not. It is based on the idea that if students know what they are supposed to learn and are provided relevant activities, they will learn it. This generalization is based on the principle of the "individuality of the learner."

Branding skills is especially important for students from disadvantaged backgrounds. Students from elite backgrounds may think the goal "skills" is too mundane and not "college level." That being said, all students, from the lowest to the highest socioeconomic level, ask, "Why do I have to learn all of this stuff?" If students perceived skills as the primary goal of their education, most would stop asking that question.

Many of my students have made the shift, changing the primary purpose of their college education from high grades to practicing and improving skills for both their careers and citizenship. Once they have done that, they are ready to deal with curriculum bloat and make their college education more relevant.

A skills coach also has to evaluate students on a continuing basis. The evaluation should always be formative, which means its purpose is to help students improve their skills. Only sometimes should it be used for grades or should it be, as the educational professionals call evaluation, "summative." Summative grades are required by the formal education system you are paid by, but the purpose of the skills coach is to motivate and guide practices.

The skills approach is not just relevant to the "do well" part of our education missions. It is also relevant to the "do good" part. While students who buy into the skills approach to their education do so for their desire to do well, the same skills are necessary to work for government and the nonprofit sector. Without the 10 skill sets, they cannot perform the tasks of effective citizens.

In the last 20 years, university leaders have also become more explicit about the duty to produce good citizens. A total of 562 university presidents signed a draft titled "The Presidents' Declaration on the Civic Responsibility of Higher Education," created in 1999 and still on the Campus Compact website today. It helped drive the movement toward community service, but most of the movement was about the spirit of wanting to give back and abstract discussions of what made good citizens. It was not about effectiveness and efficiency.

In 2000, I found myself on *Larry King Live*. In discussing my book *How You Can Help: An Easy Guide to Doing Good Deeds in Your Everyday Life*, Larry asked, "Why did you write this book?"

"To provide people with citizenship skills," I answered.

"Citizenship skills?" he said incredulously.

Today, the incredulity continues. Among conservatives, citizenship education is mostly about institutions and the Constitution. Among liberals, citizenship education is mostly about social justice. On all sides, the content in various forms of ideological spin colors textbooks and tests.

Currently, the goals of citizenship education are too much about learning dogma, or telling students what to think, and too little about how to think. We professors need to help our students acquire the 10 skill sets and then let them decide what candidates and policies they want to support or oppose.

Commitment to the skills approach is based on the idea that if students accept the 10 skill sets, they will be able to make their own decisions on the appropriateness of social and political institutions and on policies proposed by pundits. As a teacher, you will not need to tell them whether order or social justice is under threat. They will decide for themselves.

If you look at the 10 skill sets, you will easily see how many of the skills could improve our society if more people practiced them, working for their own self-interest and to improve society. Anyone who has ever attended a city council, school board, or town board meeting knows how such skills are in very short supply and how politicians can use the absence of these skills to their advantage.

Good people skills are as important for a functioning democracy as understanding the Constitution. Citizens also need to have the ability to gather information, use simple quantitative skills, ask and seek answers to the right questions, and problem solve. These skills should be at the heart of the mission of education in any democratic society. Citizens need them when they want to vote, improve their local community, or try to influence politicians.

Citizens have to seek up-to-date and vetted information to check the facts provided by politicians, governmental officials, other citizens, and lobby groups. They have to make sense out of numbers and simple statistics. When a politician says the tax rate has gone down, the citizen needs to understand that taxes may not have gone down.

Asking and answering the right questions is even more critical. To do so requires detecting nonsense, paying attention to detail, applying knowledge to specific questions, and evaluating actions and policies. Problem-solving skills enable citizens to ask supporters of a new policy, "What's the problem and how do you know it exists?"—a useful exercise for all when a policy is under consideration. Without these skills, citizens are at the mercy of those who use rhetoric in the place of reason.

These skills are also critical for a citizen's ability to follow the law and to accept the responsibilities of citizenship. Skills like Attention to Detail, Searching for Information, and Asking and Answering the Right Questions are essential for complying with government regulations, paying taxes, or traveling out of the country as well as for using government programs like Medicare, Medicaid, and Social Security.

As a skills coach, you not only help students prepare for careers. You also help them build their capacity to participate in the democratic process in a responsible and reasonable way. Professors should teach students how to think about and act in civil society rather than what ideology to follow. If they don't do that, there is no justification for an undergraduate degree program.

Skills coaches are on duty every time they interact with their students, regardless of the context. In that sense, they are a little like religious leaders who help their members in whatever context they interact with them. Keep this in mind as you read the following chapters—your role as a skills coach should shine through your work as an advisor and a boss.

Your emphasis on skills will help you to bond with your students. Once they realize that developing their skills is a central part of a college education and you are there to help them do just that, they will see you as an asset helping them rather than as an authority they're required to please. You will be well on your way to becoming a happy professor.

Chapter Four

Advisor

> We are asking advisers to do more and more.
> —Michael Anft, author of *Students Needs Have Changed: Advising Must Change, Too*

Students usually see faculty for the first time to get help in choosing courses or a major or minor. They are frequently freshmen or have been sent by one of their friends or a professional advisor to get advice because they are facing the need to make decisions soon on courses or programs.

They may see the meeting in the narrow terms of advice about courses and majors, but the meeting should have two overarching purposes: to help them get the skills and experiences they need in college, and to give them a starting point to think about careers and citizenship roles once they graduate.

THE SKILLS AND EXPERIENCE LIGHTHOUSE

Students who first contact you should receive your help as a skills coach. You should help them with their time management and communication skills specifically. Use their emails to assess their communications skills. If they start their email with "Hey" or misspell your name, correct them. If they write long paragraphs, tell them to use bullets in the future. If they say they want to meet and don't indicate their availability, send them an email saying when you are available and ask them to clearly indicate when they are. If they email back and don't include the email string, tell them to always include the email string.

Although these tactics may lose some students, most will comply and some will apologize. Some will even thank you. A few will never contact you again, which you can consider evidence that they are not ready for your advising.

Some may view this as harsh and uncaring. Maybe they are right, but the benefits outweigh the risk. Try to move students from helpless children to developing adults. You need to be direct because you are busy, and they are even busier. You have their attention for a very brief time, so strike while the iron is hot.

It sometimes hurts you and your students to be a coach. But how much more would you be hurting them if they wrote disorganized emails when contacted by an employer for a great job?

When a meeting is set, tell them to be prepared. You don't want them to open the conversation with "Tell me what courses I should take or what I should major in." Inform them that the appointment is for 15 minutes so they know they need to be organized to make the visit useful.

You can't assess their competence on most of the 10 skill sets at an initial meeting, but you can start to assess a few, like oral communication and other people skills. Ask them about their experiences. Always check for Microsoft Excel competence by asking if they have used Excel. Excel is crucial for entry-level internships and part-time jobs. It will also give you a clue about the strength of their high school, their comfort with computers, and their parental background. The conversation will also reveal their strength in skill set 9, Asking and Answering the Right Questions, and skill set 10, Solving Problems.

During the first meeting, the student needs to demonstrate their understanding of the requirements to graduate. This is very easy—just ask them how many more credits they need to graduate. If they have no clue and can't even guess, read them the riot act: Tell them that they need to take responsibility for their own education. Their future debt and the number of credit hours left toward graduation are two numbers they should know.

Students from disadvantaged backgrounds, regardless of where they are from and no matter what their race, need all the help they can get on the 10 skill sets. They have weak networks, little understanding of how undergraduate education works, and little focus.

Most of these students have been damaged by the education system because they have been C or B students but frequently have been told they are A students. They are worried they will not get a job because they are not "top" students and they are doing much worse in college than they did in high school. They want to go to law or graduate school but aren't getting the grades, and they are usually depressed and vulnerable to not finishing college or finishing with huge debt and few job opportunities.

You should explain to them that if they get the 10 skill sets, they are better off than students with high GPAs who have no people skills or think Excel is a gym class. Tell them that if they communicate well and make a nice impression, this is more valuable to many employers than students who don't have those skills but have a 3.6 GPA.

This talk is very important because they are being beaten up by most of the courses that are exercises in memorizing or manipulating abstractions. They usually don't believe they have any worth in the job market because they thought high grades were the key to career success.

They need to be told that "it's the skills, stupid." If they have a job, which most of them do, they should strive to be excellent in that job. If they work for food services, for example, tell them they should try to become a supervisor. Frequently they say, "I am a supervisor." If they do, praise them because in the path to career success, any promotion is a positive indicator. For them, it is a big deal. This gets them praise. They don't think they are a winner, but their boss thinks they are. If they are not supervisors, tell them to do what it takes to become one.

This applies to off-campus work during the academic year or in the summer. One student made $10,000 selling vacuum cleaners door to door but couldn't figure out a career path. That was an easy one. Obviously, companies would be looking to hire him in sales. He obtained a job with a staffing firm finding new clients and is doing fine. One student was a manager of a McDonald's at 19; she now is a partner in a top consulting firm.

It's the ones who have little job experience who make things difficult. They don't want to get a job on campus because it might hurt their grades, or they never worked in high school for the same reason. Maybe their peers back home don't work. That has to change if they want help.

Some students from wealthier backgrounds lack job experience. They are subsidized by their parents and encouraged to take enrichment programs, which could prevent them from working during the school year or during the summer. These enrichment experiences may help develop skills and perhaps even career exploration. However, working a summer anywhere is preferred because students who are paid have bosses who want performance.

A similar problem occurs for students who work during their summers as a camp counselor or a lifeguard. Unless they move into management, these kinds of jobs may help with some people skills but they will not allow students to explore careers. More serious than this lack of relevant experience is the real possibility that the student does not want to grow up. They may not be ready for it, which is not the end of the world but is merely a factor to consider when advising.

Give them motivation and advice on how to get a summer internship not in entertainment or sports but in something like the car rental industry. Enterprise has an excellent paid summer internship program where hard work and good people skills will result in a full-time job with good mobility within the company.

One student from Queens who took about six years to graduate came to see me (actually crying) in his fifth year and said he was worried that his grades were not high enough to get into law school. He was worried he could not get a job. He was advised to apply to Enterprise for a summer internship, which he did, and graduate from Syracuse University as soon as he could, which meant not worrying about his GPA. He did so well in his summer internship that the unit where he interned hired him after he graduated, and a year later he was managing one of the locations.

Students from disadvantaged backgrounds need extra time because their support groups tend to tell them the more education they get, the better. The sentence "I will be the first one in my family to graduate from college" carries with it the idea that all college graduates do well, when this is likely only if students develop skills and explore careers through real-world experiences.

Many disadvantaged students respond positively to the experience-and-skills idea. They thought something was wrong with them because they found many of their classes useless and uninspiring. They had trouble earning As and visualizing how they would use what they learned in their careers. The wealthy students whose parents have college degrees know they just need to suck it up and get through the drill. The rest of students find the disconnect between the majority of the coursework and what will be their future disconcerting.

Give students a lighthouse in the chaotic sea of undergraduate education. They should focus on gaining basic skills required for success not just in careers but in citizenship. They should also use experiences to see what kinds of jobs they would like in what areas. They should take classes that are hands on and choose their summer and part-time jobs and extracurricular activities to practice their skills. That gives them the direction to make sense out of the competing messages and lack of focus on skills that are inherent in undergraduate education, especially in the liberal arts.

The experience can come from volunteer activities, jobs on or off campus, or internships that will build their skills and their feel for what they want to do for a living. Discuss with students what types of activities outside of class they are involved in and how they will build skills and explore careers. It's ideal to have at least one leadership position, like manager of a recreation program or president or treasurer of a club sports team. Encourage them to cut down on the number of organizations they play a role in so they can get to these leadership positions.

When the topic of fraternities and sororities comes up, many are surprised to hear that Greek life provides tremendous leadership opportunities. Nearly all employers value leadership and people skills, and becoming a leader in a Greek organization is evidence of practicing these skills. Students will tell you that Greek life also provides contacts and networking, which is true, but networking is not as important as skills in the long run. Networking may get them their first job, but without some strength in all 10 skill sets, they will be losers.

You should be aggressive about their finances. Ask them if they will have debt when they graduate. If they tell you they don't know, ask them when are they going to take responsibility for their future. If they tell you their parents take care of the finances, tell them they are treating you like a child and not helping you become an adult. To give them a clear idea of what debt from college means, tell them that for each $10,000 in debt they accrue they will pay $100 a month for 10 years. That usually serves as a wakeup call.

Lower-middle-class and poor students who are not substantially funded through need-based aid need extra help on how to reduce debt. They are building debt, sometimes as much as $100,000. These same students will ask if they should take a summer program overseas that will add another $5,000 to their costs. Extra summer or vacation time programs usually provide valuable learning experiences, but they increase debt and sometimes delay serious career exploration. See if you can get them to see the tradeoffs.

Check to see if they can graduate a semester or a year early for two reasons. The most obvious is that students should have a little debt as possible on graduation. Debt will impact their job decisions and will reduce their standard of living for many years. The other reason is that some students coming to college with a high number of credits from high school are not into college life as a form of summer camp and are ready for the real world. They also find it frustrating to be around people who don't want to grow up. For these students, being in college is like being in the minor leagues. Playing in the majors is a better way to develop skills than playing in the minors.

FOUR USEFUL CONTINUUMS

Once you have accepted that skills gained through experience are key to undergraduate education, you are ready to deal with some more complex problems of undergraduates. You may want to use all or part of these four continuums:

1. Know-how–Knowledge
2. Bart Simpson–Bill Gates
3. Do Good–Do Well
4. People–Information

Students should think about their future by placing themselves on each of the four continuums and deciding where they want to be in the future. As they get closer to graduation, there are other continuums they might use such as live near family–don't live near family, work–life, and high risk–low risk. Stay away from these questions initially; they are not as important for most students who are trying to make sense of their college experience.

The Know-how–Knowledge Continuum

"Although I loved math and did well my first year at Syracuse, I completely lost interest in the upper levels of math. I understood two and three dimensions, but trying to understand fourth and fifth dimensions went right over my head," said one student. He probably thought math would give him the tools to perform well in various careers, but he also realized that learning for its own sake had limitations.

This example illustrates that while some students want to learn for the sake of learning (knowledge), more want to learn tools they can apply (know-how). It is not an all-or-nothing question for most students. In this case, the student realized as he took more courses that he didn't want to become an academic mathematician. Each student has a limit to how much they want to learn for the sake of learning and how much they want to learn because it can be useful to them. Knowing where they are on that continuum is important for advising students.

If they are on the know-how end, they choose coursework that increases skills, and they should allocate more time to experiences outside the traditional classroom. If they are on the knowledge end, they will usually say that they love learning. This is music to the ears of most faculty. It should be a warning siren in your case.

Students who love to learn everything will be in your office the second semester of their senior year saying they don't know what they want to do after graduation. The obvious choice for learning lovers is to go to graduate school and become professors. They may choose some kind of post-graduate scholarship, like a Fulbright or a program like Teach for America, AmeriCorps, or the Peace Corps. The latter three programs are better than the first, especially if one of them leads to a possible career, as Teach for America does.

The point is that they should have been thinking about this in their sophomore year, not the second semester of their senior year. Many never think of the know-how–knowledge continuum until it's too late. It is only when they get near the point that they may have to pay their bills that they start thinking about careers.

Most students should be somewhere in the middle of the know-how–knowledge continuum. Some students are so committed to "It's the skills, stupid" that they choose not to broaden their knowledge base. For cultural and performance reasons, they would be better off with broader knowledge, if only because they would be less boring to some of their coworkers and bosses. Most students who want to learn for the sake of learning are heading for more debt and confusion. If they are headed to an academic career, they are following a high-risk and high-cost path. Those students who love learning may be pursuing academic dreams. They should weigh the risks, benefits, and costs. They should evaluate themselves on doing well in research and publishing. Many of them think a college professor's main job is teaching (when it generally is not).

If the student wants to be an academic but does not want to do an honors thesis or major distinction project, suggest that they had better change their plans. A big writing project is a way to test commitment and competence for a wannabe PhD.

The Bart Simpson–Bill Gates Continuum

Almost as important as where the student stands on the know-how–knowledge continuum is where they stand on the continuum from the lazy and irresponsible Bart Simpson to the very energetic and hardworking Bill Gates. This Bart Simpson–Bill Gates continuum may have no basis in heavy duty research, but it should.

The key question is how much of what they do is an investment in their future, and how much of it is for fun? Bill Gates was so into working for his future career, he could not be bothered to stay at Harvard. Conversely, Bart Simpson is like Alfred E. Neuman of *Mad* magazine fame, whose most-remembered statement is "What, me worry?"

The Bart Simpson–Bill Gates continuum discussion is always necessary. Students who are on the Simpson end are not ready for much help. They need to realize that the Bart Simpson choice is not going help them prepare for the future. If they remain wedded to that choice, you need to figure out if you want to give them your time.

When told that they are too close to Bart, many will say they are going to change. If they say they are going to change, tell them words are not action and to report back when they can demonstrate a new commitment. If they disagree that they are like Bart or say college is time for fun, tell them to come back to you when they wake up.

To ease the blow and also to indicate that they are making bad choices, tell them that it doesn't mean they will be losers their entire life. At some point, they will wake up and take responsibility for their education and their future. It just might not happen until they are 30. The wealthy students are not bothered by delayed adulthood because they know their family will bail them out until they grow up. For the majority of students, they need to see the urgency.

You may see this approach as harsh, but efficiency is an important factor in advising large numbers of students. Many factors can lead students to being like Bart, including personal and family problems, drugs and alcohol, and peers who want them to fail. There is not much you can do as an advisor for an 18-year-old who wants to be Bart Simpson. Your one shot is to get them to think more about the future and less about the present.

Too many faculty members tend to view most students as Bart or close to it. Carrying this assumption around in their daily lives can be a major contributing cause of unhappiness in teaching. Happy teachers should always know, when meeting a new student, that their being on the Bart Simpson end of the continuum is not a permanent barrier. They should also know when they are running into a brick wall.

The Do Good–Do Well Continuum

Students will frequently say that they are not sure what career they want to have or even to explore. It is best always to start with the question "Do you want to do well or do good?"

Students see a "do good" career as working for a nonprofit, in a helping profession like teaching or social work, or for a government organization. Few see working in corporations as doing good. They almost never say they want to work in a traditional business job. A "do well" career indicates that they think that making money is the main concern. This goal can range from enough money to have a family and a middle-class life to being really rich.

Most students will say "Both," which seems to be the preferred answer. Faculty should have as their goal students who think about the trade-offs between a doing good and a doing well career.

If students choose the middle of the continuum, they need to plan to do well ahead of planning to do good. If they are on the do well side, feel free to tell them that you are not interested in helping selfish little brats. They should pursue the twin goals of careers and citizenship. Citizenship means thinking and acting in the public interest, even if it is only to make a little piece of the world better while in college.

If they choose the do good side of the continuum, you should help them see whether or not they are blowing smoke. Quite a few say they want to do good and mean it. They say they want to join Teach for America or the Peace Corps or take a position in a government or nonprofit career. They are usually already working in community-service activities. For those students who say they want to do good, probe to see if it is the normal reflex action from being conditioned since they were in kindergarten to save the world or if they really mean it based on what they have already done.

The reality for do-gooders is that 75% or more of the jobs in America are in the private sector, so if they want to do good they better be ready for low salaries and a lot of aggravation. They don't have to be Mother Teresa, but they do have to demonstrate the capacity for real sacrifice to work to make society better.

To check, ask the proclaimed do-gooders if they want to be poor and are willing to sacrifice. That usually leads to a recant and switch from "do good" to "do both." For those students who really want a life of sacrifice, make sure they see all the benefits and costs of a do good career. Perhaps only 10% are actually committed to a life and career in doing good, but even many of these will ultimately go for the money.

In either case, move on to asking them what kind of career they might pursue after college. The naive do-gooders will say something like "I want to protect the environment" or "I want to improve urban education." Help them realize that a career is not a life goal. If they say "protect the environment" and hate science, suggest they sell solar panels, which is not exactly what they will have in mind. If they say they want to improve urban education, ask them if they want to be a teacher. If they say they want to change educational policy but don't want to teach for a few years, you should point out that we have too many people fixing things they know little about.

For all your advisees, bring up the idea of graduating early as a way to grow up and save money. Many students bring advance credit in with them and can get out in 3 or 3 1/2 years, but few think about it. They should at least think about the benefit of leaving college for the real world earlier than they expected. They may lose some learning opportunities, but they need to think in terms of cost and benefits. Besides, they will develop more skills and learn more about what career they want to follow in the real world than they will in another year of college.

For most students, despite their complaints about stress, undergraduate college is more like a very expensive summer camp than an opportunity to prepare for their future. For poor students, it is living in an upper-middle-class environment and an escape from where they came from. As long as these students focus on skills and minimize debt, they can enjoy the years in college. However, they also need to be prepared to pursue careers in which they can support themselves while living in an upper-middle-class environment. If they don't develop skills and explore careers, they won't be prepared.

The People–Information Continuum

After taking care of the basics through these three continuums, you are ready to talk about what kind of career students would prefer to start with. That question is premature until the student has thought through where they are on the know-how–knowledge, Bart Simpson–Bill Gates, and do good–do well continuums.

There are many other continuums students might use, such as travel–don't travel, 40 hour work week–80 hour work week, and high risk–low risk. However, the most important to start with is the people–information continuum. Does the student want to work primarily with people or analyze information in some way? Although all careers involve both, the distinction is important. As students move up their career ladders, they will be doing more of both.

Some students will say they like using Excel and providing memos and presentations on policy choices, but others say they don't want to be chained to a desk "just making graphs." Other students choose the people option because they like to interact with people individually or in groups. This continuum is key to where the student will end up going. The information pole leads to administrative and consulting jobs and professions like law and accounting. The people pole leads to teaching, clinical-type work directly with people, and, most likely, sales.

Many students recoil at the idea of sales because it is not viewed as something you go to college for, or they suffer from the idea of the snake-oil salesman. These views are unfortunate since sales is the hardest of all professions and requires the highest level of most skills. Moreover, whatever they do, students will be in sales in one way or another. Sales is also a highly paid field and rarely requires an advanced degree.

Your advising plays a pivotal role in helping students prepare for a career and citizenship. It is much more than guiding students to take a specific major and what courses to take. It is acquiring the role that students want and need for their decision to spend time and money on your institution. You are not the only resource for advising that students need, and you may decide to not embrace the multiple tasks required by the role as described in this chapter. That is okay, but that decision will reduce one of the biggest sources of happiness in undergraduate teaching: helping students reach their career and citizenship potential after college. You have the opportunity, through the use of these four continuums, to help students get past the confusion caused by the college curriculum bazaar they face. You instead show them the enormous array of opportunities they are offered.

Chapter Five

Boss

If you think your teacher is tough, wait till you get a boss.

—Bill Gates

If students are to be treated as young adults rather than children, they should be put in a position that will be a major source of challenge and opportunity in their careers. That position is getting used to having a boss and working to keep their job and get promoted. This is also true for volunteer positions. You can act as a boss in a variety of ways.

Students who want to develop skills need coaching, practicing through experience, and advising. Apprenticeship learning combines the three. It is superior to any other form of learning. The term "boss" means both coaching and mentoring, but with consequences. It is powerful for many reasons. It has grades and money behind it and signals an acceptance by the apprentices that they are in a learning relationship. The problem is that in the modern world, where there are so many students and so few mentors, there are not enough apprenticeships.

For me, the boss-employer relationship gives apprenticeships for about 70 students a semester. Students are "paid" with graded credit or, for the best students, with money. They learn to do what is needed and what will also give them experiences to improve their skills and present an impressive relationship. All they have to do is perform the designated jobs.

The apprentice relationship has been revolutionary for students in the program. Students produce what clients estimate is at least $100,000 worth of work per academic year in the form of research studies, administrative work, and educational activities. The outcome for government and nonprofit organizations in the local county, as well as for selected places around the world, is not the primary purpose of these activities. The primary purpose is to create a real-world performance opportunity for and metric of the students, but the by-product is productive community engagement for the agencies.

The bossing experience is provided in four different ways. All of them tie together, and once students do well at one level, they move up the food chain. This gives the program the resources to take on projects and make changes that would never be possible otherwise. At any given time, I employ student "employees" in the following areas:

1. Undergraduate teaching assistants
2. The Community Link Program
3. Student-run projects under my supervision
4. Office staff

The first and most impactful bossing activity is the use of undergraduate teaching assistants (UTAs) in a freshman course. This opportunity is open to 20 students per semester who the preceding semester had taken a course to be a UTA.

This use of UTAs led to using undergraduates to do as much work as they could to help in our various projects. From about 40 UTAs a year, several who want to work in the future are recruited, similar to how corporations provide internships or hire people out of college for a one- or two-year stints.

The second format of the bossing approach is the Community Link Program taught for the course Policy Analysis and Presentation at Syracuse. It is the second "methods" course in the policy studies major, building on a basic introduction to data analysis. Instead of providing lectures and artificial homework assignments as usual, the boss approach requires applying learning methods to real-world clients.

The students, who see themselves as working for a consulting firm, are assigned a client. They meet with their assigned client for 30 minutes in the first class and get a contract signed. The clients are told to think of the students as professional who are being compensated. In most cases, the clients are happy with the product they receive.

Students have to deal with their professor as the boss, which means taking direction but also working as a junior colleague. Students provide drafts when the boss tells them what to fix, but sometimes the boss changes his mind when he sees the changes because that is what bosses do, and the project is a process. Sometimes the students argue, which is basically a good thing unless the boss says, "Just do what I say," in which case the student has to accept the command.

The boss approach may be viewed as harsh, uncaring, and whatever else you want to think. It contrasts to the approach many professors take, but this approach asks the professor to place the value of the product to the client above the feelings of the student.

A third role of the boss is as an entrepreneur. An idea for a project or research activity may emerge that the professor would like to see students undertake and, for the most part, own. The professor encourages a single student or a group of volunteers to earn credit by pursuing the idea. The professor can play advisor or, if credit or employment is involved, be the "investor" who could pull the plug. Some of these ideas work out, but most don't survive over the long run. Frequently the professor may decide to remove his or her support and recommend killing the project. The angst created by that decision introduces in real terms the principle that it's okay to cut your losses.

One project at Syracuse University that has survived for four years is a program where undergraduates become certified to help people complete their income tax form so they can receive money from the federal government under the earned income tax credit (EITC). This came about after a lecturer mentioned in class the EITC and how many poor people did not take advantage of it, and a student said she wanted to lead the project. She had already been an outstanding student and was a UTA for a junior-level course. She organized it by working with the IRS, which is enough of a challenge, and with local nonprofits, which is even more of a challenge. She recruited about 15 students, trained someone to replace her, and talked an economics professor into giving one credit attached to a course he was teaching. She taught many students about public policy and about poverty—or, rather, those students learned about policy and poverty as a result of their experiences.

Every year something new comes up at Syracuse University, usually in helping Syracuse City high schools do a better job by providing enrichment activities after school. Strong leaders emerge, and students in the freshman courses join to help, and eventually these students take on leadership roles.

These projects sometimes fail because of unclear priorities and irresponsible volunteers, but failure is a key to learning about leadership and management. On some occasions, students might learn about power. A student who ran an after-school program very successfully decided he wanted to make it an independent student organization, which is rarely a good idea. The professor told him no, but the student kept doing it anyway, and his team complained about his "big head." However, since the professor was paying the student and providing other financial support for the project, he had leverage and eventually fired the student. The student probably still thinks he did nothing wrong, but perhaps he and those who were with him saw the need to listen to those with money and power.

A final and more intense boss role is for students who work in the professor's office with staff members. The professor's administrative assistant does the direct supervision. These students learn to work under a chain of command that emanates from the professor's authority. There can be a lot of confusion and tension. However, students learn a great deal about office relationships so when they get to the real world they recognize their vital importance.

The boss is both a manager and a leader. Those two roles are different, requiring different skills and functions. Students need to learn not only to deal with their immediate supervisors but also to see good and bad leadership skills. While the primary purpose of having students "work" for the professor as a boss is to help them cope with the idea that they will need to do what the boss wants, there is a secondary benefit. They observe the professor's behavior and hopefully avoid many weaknesses they have as a manager and a leader.

Students working for a professor, no matter what the extrinsic payoffs, expand the resources and educational impact available to the professor. New ideas, whether to improve a section of a course or to make the university or city better, can be examined beyond abstract discussions with real consequences other than a grade. The professor's amount of time on such tasks is reduced because the students do the time-consuming work. The professor gets more effective classes, a publication, or occasionally cash to share with the students. What could be a better way to be happy than educating undergraduates and making the world better simultaneously?

Part II

Strategies

The following chapters introduce five broad strategies that I incorporate in my teaching. I use these strategies when designing, delivering, and evaluating the courses I teach. They have had a revolutionary impact on my teaching, not just with respect to career and citizenship but to whatever content I provide. They may not be the strategies you now employ or even want to employ, but try one or more of them out. Your students will see themselves as junior colleagues, and you will be happy to have their help and counsel.

Chapter Six

Andragogy, Not Pedagogy

> The art of handling university students is to make oneself appear, and this almost ostentatiously, to be treating them as adults.
> —Arnold Joseph Toynbee, *Experiences*

Some education researchers have drawn a sharp distinction between teaching children (pedagogy) and teaching adults (andragogy). In pedagogy, children see the teacher as an authority figure with complete knowledge and power. Children will learn what they learn because the teacher tells them to do it. The closed trinity of lectures-readings-tests dominates the classroom. The primary motivation is the grade, and the content is to be stored in the children's minds in case an occasion for application comes up.

In contrast, adults want to learn what they want to learn, not what the teacher tells them to learn. Consequently, adults are independent of what they learn. In andragogy, learning occurs primarily through experience. The role of the trinity of lectures-readings-tests is secondary. Application is more important than remembering, repeating, and comparing theories and concepts.

Despite the fact that undergraduates better fit the description of an adult, most faculty members and administrators still use the term "pedagogy." This is not just a verbal slip; it's a Freudian slip. It represents the framework too many faculty members use when they define and execute their teaching strategies: They treat their students as children because that is the way they were treated.

Pedagogy has had a devastating impact on teaching. Andragogy, on the other hand, as described in the 1960s by the originator of the term, Malcolm Knowles, requires the teacher recognize that students know what they want to learn and how they want to learn. Adult students cannot be bullied into learning whatever the teacher decides needs to be learned.

The "individuality of the learner" runs counter to the prevailing idea of the teacher as the knowledge provider. The principle of the "individuality of the learner" is required for the same reason that democracy is preferred over autocracy in our political and social institutions. Not only does the principle lead to more engaged students who will have better career and citizenship skills and attitudes, it will also provide relationships between faculty members and students that are less dictatorial.

The "individuality of the learner" not only directly threatens the power relationship between the faculty and the undergraduate, it also raises the question of how much professors can educate undergraduates. If we are talking about changing the behavior of learners with respect to careers and citizenship, nature and nurture are far more important than formal education.

Undergraduates should be treated as young adults rather than as children. It enables professors and students to collaborate on mutual learning. Professors never need to worry about control over their students because most students who buy into the goals of their classes take responsibility for their own learning. Yes, there are always a few who never get on the train, but that is their choice.

Andragogy means that students see you as their coach and themselves as apprentices. They know the coach is helping them with their careers and their role as citizens. They are signing on to a contractual relationship where they are treated as adults who share a goal with their professor. Every idea and suggestion in this book rests on the grand strategy of treating undergraduates as adults. Undergraduates should not be treated as if they value education as an ornament, even though too many students and their parents do just that. If you want to change behavior so your students can achieve their personal goals and strengthen their commitment to citizenship, always ask yourself, "Is this about my students, or about me and the institutions that support me?"

Treating students as children is the road to unhappiness. For those of you who have children, you know the level of anxiety that increases year after year as your level of control diminishes. You feel a responsibility for helping them have a happy future, but as each year passes you have less and less control. Responsibility without control is a source of great unhappiness for most parents, especially if they are delusional about the amount of control they have. Treating students as adults reduces the responsibility you have for their success and allows you to be happy with the effects of your teaching.

If you see your students as adults, you accept the fact that you have little or no control over what they choose to do or become. The stress and anxiety disappear, and you embrace the profound the truth that you can lead a horse to water but you can't make it drink. Just think about how happy parents are when they feel they can treat their children as adults, and how sad they are when they have to treat their grown adults as children.

Chapter Seven

The Five Laws of the Minimalist

The best is the enemy of the good.

—Voltaire

The vast majority of faculty members are maximalists: They want their students to learn as much as possible. Minimalists want students to learn the basics. A solid grounding in the basics can help all students. Then those who are interested and capable can go as far as they want. The professional educationists call this "scaffolding." You wouldn't create a building without scaffolding; why would you help students develop skills and acquire knowledge by starting at the top?

Maximalist professors tend to leave the majority of the class behind as they seek to stimulate themselves by talking only to the best and the brightest. They assume that all students have the basic skills and can apply the basic concepts, and they give high grades to those students who have learned the most.

Maximalist professors allocate more time to covering more content than minimalist professors, who trade more content for more practice. Since the "top" is undefined, professors have trouble deciding what the standard should be. The one thing they are sure of is that "standard" is beyond the basic level.

Minimalist professors take the opposite approach. They want students to reach a basic level. The happy professor's standards focus on the 10 skill sets presented in chapter 3 as well as on the basic terminology of the subject matter. Nature and nurture will determine how far students will go up the steps. The minimalist strategy is to get them on the first couple of steps so they can travel as far as they want to go. Most professors want to pull students up the steps so they can have students who will stimulate them.

Minimalists are happy to see how many steps the students can complete without their help. Happy professors need to be minimalists when educating today's undergraduates for careers and citizenship. They need to have standards that are the most basic skills and knowledge necessary for a reasonable chance to do well and do good. The minimalist's criteria are driven by what the student will do in the real world, both now and in the not-too-distant future.

The following five simple "laws" of the minimalist are likely to strike you as strange and maybe impossible to follow. Try one or two sometime. You may be surprised how much they provide a new way to get your students to learn how to do well and do good—not to mention how much stress and unhappiness they will reduce for you as a professor.

MINIMALIST LAW NUMBER 1: REDUCE EDUCATIONAL GOALS

The K–12 curriculum is one mile wide and one inch deep. Undergraduate curriculum is one million miles wide and perhaps one-half inch deep. Curriculum bloat, where every academic discipline gets its "fair" share enlarged by programs designed to attract more students, continues to grow. It prevents students from getting what they need for careers and citizenship.

To illustrate, just look at the teaching of mathematics. Many students hate and fear mathematics because they are forced to learn topics that have little utility and are only accessible to the mathematically gifted. They will need a certain level of mathematical comprehension to understand the news, work in business and government, and manage their own lives. They rarely get to practice these simple operations during college.

For example, although students are introduced to absolute numbers, rates, and percentages before high school, students in college typically can't differentiate between these three types of measures. Many of them appear to have never heard the terms, despite having already taken a college-level statistics course.

The reason for these weaknesses and the lack of other simple skills and concepts is that no subjects are presented or practiced enough for students to master their use. Students are forced by their teachers to march to the next set of materials. Students need to practice these basic types of measures in a variety of contexts for a substantial amount of time to use them properly.

The pressures against practice and mastery and toward introducing more topics have become a major tension in course design at all levels. This is the result of a few factors. First, associations and others push for their latest fad or product to be included in the curriculum, contributing to bloat. Second, students don't like to practice. They find it boring, as do the professors who have to manage and monitor the practice. Third, different student backgrounds require different amounts of time devoted to practice.

The trouble this causes for the future of our college graduates is clearly evidenced in most students' lack of Microsoft Excel skills. This is one specific example, but there are many other skill and content areas where students have poor mastery. Students are given so much to learn that they can't discern what is important and what is not. When it comes to content, maximalists think "the more the better," which is why students don't practice what is important for careers and citizenship.

The most effective way to contribute to better student mastery is by providing learning through experience, where students produce work for some kind of "client." However, it is difficult for students to get high-quality experiences that will contribute to their skills and knowledge. Grades in coursework only begin to assess the ability of the student to master the content or skill.

Many skills—for example, basic statistical analysis, clear and concise writing to communicate, and one-on-one communication—are given too little class time because they need to be practiced and require faculty to do mundane things. In addition, faculty introduce too much material in an effort to give students every concept they deem necessary. Tests and essays are intended to gauge students' retention and understanding of technical concepts, but in reality, the students practice triage. They select what they think the instructors are looking for and take away little of lasting value from their coursework.

Creating courses and programs to "cover" a subject is the fertilizer theory of education. The course "covers" the material such as you would spread fertilizer over the lawn. If you cover the entire lawn, you have completed the task. You will see a nice lawn. If you cover your subject matter for your students, what will you see?

MINIMALIST LAW NUMBER 2: TEACH BY THE 10% PRINCIPLE

Professors need to accept that fact that nature and nurture determine skill levels and understanding of the world far more than lectures and required activities. Professors are pleased when alumni write testimonials saying how a professor changed their life. The reality is the student changed their life; the professor should only take credit for 10%. For a professor, that 10% is getting students to see what they need to learn so the students can take their own steps toward learning it.

The 10% principle of the minimalist is related to the advice provided for advising in chapter 4. In advising, your only responsibility is to suggest the paths the student may take. It is the student's responsibility to do the rest.

You are not responsible for how much students learn or how skilled they are. The 10% minimalist law is based on the Serenity Prayer used by Alcoholics Anonymous and first articulated by Reinhold Niebuhr:

> God, grant me the serenity to accept the things I cannot change,
> Courage to change the things I can,
> And wisdom to know the difference.

The 10% principle will bring you happiness in your undergraduate teaching. The Serenity Prayer will bring you happiness in the rest of your life.

MINIMALIST LAW NUMBER 3: NEVER USE CURVES

Professors show their maximalist attitudes most clearly when they choose to use curves to determine letter grades. The idea behind the curve is that the more the student gets right on a test or assignment, the higher the grade. The basics are ignored so that the student's score reflects the amount of stuff apparently learned. In using a curve, maximalist professors are admitting that they don't know what their standards are. They will reward the students who apparently learned the most.

The curve is a perfect protection for the maximalist professor because the students' performances yield numbers that can be fit to a normal distribution, which absolves the professor of the appearance of bias and provides a strong base for dealing with complainers. They don't like living with doubt, which is inherent in making decisions that affect their students' lives. "The curve made me do it" is an iron-tight excuse.

Academics have written books and articles on the use of curves. Those who support curves are maximalists who believe the more the better. They tend to use multiple-choice tests, and they believe having students compete with each other is a great motivation for learning more stuff. It also feeds into the grading frenzy that usually gets in the way of learning.

MINIMALIST LAW NUMBER 4: IGNORE THE TRADITIONAL SEAT-TIME RULE

As maximalists, faculty members still act as if classroom seat time should meet the standard of 45 hours per credit during the semester. The formula is in many state laws, but it is not enforced. If it were, there would be no online, experiential, or independent study courses. Moreover, the 45 hours per credit is unenforceable. That would require taking attendance and punishing those who miss class, which many faculty do not do. Basically, faculty members don't police the seat-time requirement.

However, the vast majority of faculty members want to make sure that all 45 hours are full of stuff to transmit or discuss. Many complain that the 45 hours of seat time per credit is not enough to cover all the material. As noted earlier, teaching is not covering material.

Some use a workshop approach, which basically allows students to do their homework during class time. This practice allows the faculty member to coach while students are practicing. Allocated time to work on team projects is another beneficial use of seat time because all team members will be available to meet.

Faculty members like to hold office hours outside class rather than cancel class to hold individual meetings. Consider this approach. Ten minutes one-on-one discussing how to produce a better product for a specific client is much better than giving ten generic tips to twenty students at once. In an individual meeting, tips will be relevant to that student, and you won't be wasting everyone else's class time.

Another reason for using class time for individual meetings is that professors have very few office hours, and students will more likely than not have a class during the professor's hours. Students sometimes feel forced to miss a class in order to meet with their professor. If office hours are during class time, there is no excuse.

Maximalists will argue that these meetings should be in addition to class time. They'll say that class time is most precious since students will be able to hear it from the horse's mouth. They will say eliminating class meetings for individual meetings is morally reprehensible. They don't accept the 10% principle or the individuality of the learner.

MINIMALIST LAW NUMBER 5: TEACH THE SAME COURSE EVERY YEAR

The arguments against a stable teaching gig—teaching the same course every year—are numerous: You will get bored. You will get stale. You will have a huge teaching burden. You will not be able to teach upper-level undergraduates, honors students, and graduate students. These challenges cannot be ignored. The challenges can be handled if you use UTAs. You will not get bored because the UTAs will entertain you. You will not get stale because the UTAs will tell you your weaknesses every day. You will not be burdened because the UTAs are your busy bees. Finally, the introductory course will run itself so you have more time for other things (see chapter 10 for further discussion of the benefits of using UTAs).

All faculty members know that until they teach a course two or three times, the course needs serious revisions. Problem solving, which is the heart of course development, takes time, repetition, and incremental revisions.

Your decision to teach the same introductory course would send a powerful learning message to your students. Teaching the same course every semester or every year helps build cohesion among students. It creates informal peer learning as previous students help their friends taking the course do well. It can build a following that will recruit students to your class, and those students will know what they are getting into. This means they will select your course instead of being forced into it or taking a chance on the unknown.

A citizen who works in K–12 education and advocates for reform once said, when discussing a reform, "It's always about the adults and never about the students." That goes double in undergraduate education. However, commitment to teach the same course every year is about the students.

Part of the reason for this is that faculty members are artists and want to do what they want to do. If you are able to teach the same course once an academic year and draw many students who basically like it, you are an artist with a following. What more could you ask for?

There is also an institutional payoff. Entry-level courses in the social sciences and humanities, and some courses in the professional schools, lack consistency across different instructors. From the students' viewpoint and the institutional requirement, this cannot be a good thing. Unless the course is offered by the same faculty members, evidence of the course's value is weak or nonexistent. The only real test of a successful course is that students express value in surveys and enrollment is either stable or increased. If a course is offered by different faculty each year, enrollment cannot be used to measure its value.

In certain fields, introductory courses are supposed to prepare students for next-level courses. If the next professor feels the students are prepared, that will indicate value. When the introductory instructor shifts frequently, the next-level professors cannot assume all the students learned the same prerequisite skills and material. These professors are not likely to suggest adjustments because they don't know who will be teaching the course next and don't want to expend the energy every time a new instructor is assigned to teach the course.

This strategy for you as a teacher is likely to run into opposition from your colleagues. They may think that since they don't want to teach the same course all the time, you shouldn't either, unless you are incompetent. Jealousy may be in play since you'd consistently be getting good reviews. They might argue that the field is changing so much you may not be keeping up with the changes. There is always pressure for what's "new" or what's "creative" in higher education. It is unfortunate that there is not equal pressure for stability and good execution.

You may not be fully appreciated, or you may be frequently criticized for pandering to students or for a lack of rigor. If you receive such criticism, ignore it. Be happy that you are playing such an important role in your students' lives.

A minimalist viewpoint releases you from the constant fear that you have not done enough to help your students succeed. You may develop a new fear that you have done too much. Balance is important, but give yourself a break from your desire to control as much as possible and you will feel much better.

Chapter Eight

Everything Is Experiential

> We cannot think first and act afterwards. From the moment of birth we are immersed in action and can only fitfully guide it by taking thought.
> —Alfred North Whitehead

The dichotomy between those who teach using the traditional trinity of lectures-readings-tests and those who practice experiential learning is a false one. Reading, taking tests, writing papers, and being dazzled by a great lecturer are experiences just as work in a science lab, team projects, community service, and internships are. The real question is, what kinds of experiences do you want to use in educating your students?

The traditional trinity is not without value in the development of skills and content knowledge and can still be part of your arsenal. The trinity should, however, be supplemented in the classroom by discussions, competitive activities like simulations and games, and team-based projects. Opportunities outside the classroom include online exercises, community-based learning, public lectures, videos, movies, chat rooms, internships, jobs, and student activities.

Implementing activities outside the trinity will improve student learning. Such activities will allow students to not spend time figuring out what you want them to learn, which violates the individuality of the learner principle. With the proper reflective activities, students decide what the lessons are themselves.

The strategy is to bring the real world into your classroom and bring the student into the real world. This strategy applies to the traditional scholarly goal of most faculty, which is to learn the discipline. If you want students to understand existing scholarship on a subject, you can have students attend lectures offered out of class or bring scholars to class who disagree with each other so the students can witness the exchange. For small and upper-division courses, team research projects that require collecting and analyzing data make sense.

If your goal is also to help students develop skills and apply concepts to do well and do good, there are many ways to give them "real" experiences inside and outside the classroom. The list below starts with the easiest to implement.

Written Assignments: Require assignments where students are writing to some real or hypothetical person other than you. As a skills coach, you can grade the paper using your own academic standards but also to the degree that the person addressed would understand the paper and find it useful. For example, in political science, the paper could be written to a local office. In English, the paper could be written to the author of a novel.

Outside Speakers in Class: Rather than setting up a speaker as an expert to be reverenced, tell the class to look at the speaker as an individual to be observed. Have the speaker begin with a brief background on themselves, talk about the subject for 30% of the time allotted, and then ask for questions. Where possible, you could ask the speaker to play a role in some type of exercise. For example, a former public official could pretend she is a mayor and then react to student proposals. This type of thing can be done for any subject where the speaker acts as judge. Your choice of speaker is important. The speaker does not have to be an expert. He or she can be someone in the community who is impacted in some way by what the students are studying and who can add to their expertise.

Toe-in-the-Water Community-Service Requirement: Require students to do five hours of community volunteer work. It does not have to be a placement on a topic they are studying. Many students enjoy the experience so much that they continue to volunteer the rest of the semester and, sometimes, the entire time they are at the university. Don't worry too much about the quality of the placement other than that the organization be open to the placement. If you do not want to make it a course requirement, you could give extra credit or at the very least provide a list of opportunities. You might require a written reflection paper. A very wealthy alumnus who has donated much to Syracuse University claims this requirement completely transformed him as a student and a person. He raised his GPA, went to law school, and, well, now he is a wealthy alumnus.

Projects for Clients: For all undergraduate fields, you can find clients within and outside the college who need help in the form of tutoring, presentations, teaching materials, and research reports. Students can work individually or in teams as part of your course requirements or for extra credit to serve the needs of the client.

To illustrate, you can create a class where government and nonprofit agencies request research projects they need for their board of directors or funders. If you offer free services to understaffed and underfunded nonprofit and government agencies, you will get many requests. You provide the students with advice and a review to help them produce a report. Students typically say this was the most important course they took from me and that the interaction with their client was as educational as writing the report. Students will speak of the report they produce for the class in job interviews, which usually results in their being hired.

You may not want to try this for a large number of clients initially. You could try it as an independent study if you find a client who needs a study done, then build a large mailing list over time to solicit projects. You can also have an entire class produce a study for a client. In this way, students not only serve the needs of the local community, they also practice their data analysis and writing skills.

Broaden Your View of Independent Study and Experience Credit: The increasing desire of students to get hands-on experience faces a serious barrier in the traditional treatment of independent study and experience-based credit in most undergraduate programs. A faculty member who specializes in the field typically must agree to sign off on a study that is intended to be an act of scholarship. Faculty have had no problem giving credit to their best students who assist them with their own research. However, that doesn't solve the problem for the bulk of students who do not want to become a professor's protégé.

The solution to the independent study problem is to have students produce products for a client within or outside the university, like those described in the section above. However, few faculty members have taken that path because they want to see a connection between their discipline and the experience. This difficulty is particularly a problem for students in the arts and sciences who might major in sociology, for example, but get a summer job at Walmart and can't find a sociology professor to see that experience as relevant to the study of sociology or to take the time to make it relevant.

There are two options that kill three birds with one stone. The first is the "skills internship." The job or internship experience does not have be in a specific academic field. Instead, the work required outside the internship itself relates to assessing and developing skills and is a "do-good activity" where the student comes up with a policy suggestion for the organization. For every 45 hours of work and accompanying online exercises, a student might receive one credit. Students usually work enough for three credits in a semester. Whether working at Dunkin' Donuts or as paid research assistants, students can make the experience one of their electives by completing the exercises.

The second is a course tied to a specific student activities office at the university such as the Office of Residence Life. Resident Advisors (RAs) are carefully selected and then provided 30–60 hours of training. The training, plus a series of outline assignments culminating in a policy proposal to improve the effectiveness of RAs, would be an example of such a course. Students can receive three hours of credit for their work. Another example of students earning academic credit for their training is working in a literacy core tutoring program. Other student activities can be incorporated in this course as well.

Think about how to adapt these ideas to your teaching activities. You could try them on an ad hoc basis through whatever credit options you might have. If your goals for the undergraduates you teach are doing well and doing good, all kinds of paths are available through experience credit.

Embracing an experiential approach in designing and delivering instruction can have a revolutionary impact on the behavior of students. For one thing, it requires students to get out of their little social media boxes and talk to adults. It can be used to teach disciplinary materials, but it also helps students practice the wide range of skills they will need as adults in their personal lives, their careers, and as citizens. Experiential education should not be viewed as a tool to use on some occasions but rather as a framework for everything you do to improve the capacity of students to do well and do good.

You may be thinking that incorporating more hands-on experience and less of the lectures-readings-tests trinity will create more work for you. It will require a different use of your time and also force you into something you don't usually do. Even finding outside speakers and getting them to do what you want can be annoying and time-consuming. Once you set up the experience, it becomes easier to implement in the future. You will develop a system to incorporate simulations, role plays, or even community service into your class with less time and effort on your part. You will spend less time preparing lectures and even grading papers. You will find it to be a powerful and efficient strategy. If you adopt the practice of using undergraduates as apprentices, you will have much less work in running experiential programs. You will find it entertaining and useful, and it will help build your understanding of individual and group behavior. Trust in this.

Chapter Nine

Evaluate Yourself

No one can make you feel inferior without your consent.
—Eleanor Roosevelt

Evaluation, whether by others or yourself, can be a source of stress and unhappiness. Don't let it be.

If you see yourself as an artist, believe in your own teaching individuality, and agree that your students have the right to individuality, your best source of evaluation is yourself. Student evaluations are always mixed and highly dependent on the grades you give. Faculty, chairs, and deans will proudly proclaim that student evaluations are flawed yet still use them in performance reviews. Given this inability to measure student career and citizenship outcomes in a systematic way, what are you to do?

Performance evaluation may work to some extent outside academia because organizations have clear goals and can obtain more concrete performance measures. However, performance evaluations are called "summative," and the results place employees on a continuum from good to bad.

The only measure that should be used for summative evaluation of faculty is how students vote with their feet. The number of students who complete your course can be a summative measure. Other outcome measures related to career and citizenship, as any competent social scientist should know, cannot be easily obtained. The idea that you can determine careers and citizenship in a rigorous way ignores the minimalist 10% principle.

The best way to look at evaluation is as a formative, not summative, exercise. It tells you what you should do to improve your teaching rather than how good you are. Department chairs and teaching committees should see evaluation as formative and minimize the role of the results in salary and promotion decisions. It is much easier to see the use of student evaluation as a basis for making suggestions for improvement.

COLLECT TESTIMONIALS

Just because businesses collect and use testimonials to increase sales should not diminish their value to you and your institution. Read and keep the notes you get from students saying how much you helped them in doing well and doing good. If you do it correctly, even C students will say they have learned a lot about what to do in the future. You don't have to put the testimonials on your website or use them as a sales pitch. Just consider them an affirmation of you as an artist. Affirmation leads to happiness.

USE STUDENT SURVEYS WISELY

Colleagues say they receive bad reviews because they have high standards, which really means "I don't give a lot of As." It's hard, but aren't professors somewhat special and able to stay out of this blatant cognitive-dissonance trap? Treat the data as information to help you improve what you do the next semester. Bad news from student surveys can lead to good news.

To learn something that will help improve your class, the sample size of your student surveys is critical. Unless you get above a 60% response rate, you are likely to have sampling bias, which limits the value of the data. This bias means the lovers and haters answer the questions, while the rest do not.

To get a high response rate, ask that a response be turned in and threaten a point deduction if one isn't. If you feel that policy is too controlling and you get a response rate of less than 70%, you probably don't give a high enough priority to evaluating your teaching.

Look at the closed-choice question numbers to get a quick view of how students felt about the course. The key is responses to the open-ended questions. Ask what was good about the course, what was bad about the course, and how to improve the course. Written comments allow you to understand the praise and criticism and to get new ideas.

FACULTY REACTIONS

While your prime evaluative advice is to listen to your students during and after the class, you could be teaching a course that "services" other courses. If so, you will want to know if your students are prepared for the next class. This may not be as simple as it sounds. In most cases, your colleagues will not tell you that students coming into their classes are unprepared. Instead, they will tell everyone else, which creates angst and miscommunication.

To avoid this confusion, ask your colleagues if your students are prepared for their next class and, if not, what is missing. A private meeting communicates that you see your job as preparing students for their classes. This may yield some changes in both courses that allow for the needed transition.

Part III

Engagement Tactics

This is the first of four sections listing specific tactics you can use. These four sections organize tactics you may follow to enjoy yourself more in your teaching.

This section will help you increase student engagement. This is, by far, the most important set of tactics in achieving your educational goals. You won't be able to help students to do well or do good if you don't engage them. The tactics, like everything I suggest in this book, are taken from my own experiences, which means they may not work for you. If that is the case, hopefully they will lead you to other ideas that get your students engaged. Engaged students are happy students who will keep you happy.

Chapter Ten

Use Undergraduate Teaching Assistants

Each one teach one.
—African American proverb originating during slavery

Undergraduate teaching assistants (UTAs) have been widely used in many fields at least since the 1980s at many prestigious universities like Duke and Cornell as well as those less well known. However, the practice remains scary for many administrators and faculty, especially those who have trouble viewing their undergraduates as adults.

The idea behind UTAs is as old as education itself. It is apprentice learning. This tactic is by far the most important road for the happy professor. It will transform everything you do as a teacher and, at the same time, make your workload more powerful and more fun. You will not have less work, but you will not have to do some of the repetitive things you now do, which means you can improve your courses and expand your educational impact. In addition, this will provide you with a set of junior colleagues with fresh ideas, unlimited energy, and perspective from having been students in the course in which they are now UTAs. Your courses will be better from the work of your junior colleagues year after year.

You will also have created your own little tribe who will help you, as it is in the students' career and citizenship interests to help you. Happiness comes from having support groups, especially if the groups increase your reach and influence.

You will be at risk of the charge that you are creating your own tribe, or worst yet, cult. Faculty will make fun of you and gossip behind your back. Students not in your tribe will accuse you of favoritism because they were not chosen or were rejected from your group. Just be welcoming, and maybe they'll fall in line. Take everything in stride.

The idea of UTAs was first introduced in chapter 4 as part of the boss role. UTAs play a major role in the development and continuous improvement of the policy studies major at Syracuse University and the gateway freshman course Introduction to the Analysis of Public Policy. At the same time, the UTAs receive extensive practice in all 38 skills as they coach six hours a week (three in pre-course meetings and three in the course). The course averages about 130 students a semester, from which there are usually 20 UTAs out of about 45 eager freshman and sophomore applicants.

By far the biggest impact of using UTAs is to transform a large lecture class so that students find it accessible, like a small class. The UTAs are the students' peers, and they have face-to-face contact with students during each class and the UTAs' office hours. The student can casually ask little things in class, like what the format of a paper should be or where to find something on the class website.

So what are the advantages of UTAs other than getting papers graded and reducing time teaching this freshman course? The advantages can be divided into two groups: benefits to the course and benefits to the UTAs.

With respect to benefits to the course for the students, the most important is creating materials and lectures that are not too much over the heads of students. Since the UTAs took the course the previous semester, they can preview lecture slides and help make them clearer and shorter. They are sources of minimalist training for the instructor.

UTAs also provide resources to further help the students. For example, they can suggest and produce a newsletter for each of the course papers that gives tips. You might not have thought of that or had the time to produce one, but your UTAs could. The following are just a few of the innovations your UTAs could provide, taken from our program at Syracuse University:

1. Outside speaker surveys: A UTA emails a survey from SurveyMonkey about the speaker and the students respond within 48 hours. A UTA provides analysis and sends it to the speaker.
2. Community-service placements: A UTA facilitates the placement and monitoring of students who have a five-hour service requirement.
3. Extra credit for going to relevant lectures: A UTA assigns extra credit for selected speeches and receives a form from students who attend.
4. Group leadership: 20 UTAs take roll and become facilitators and mentors for a group of about seven students each. They also handle problems that come up with missing students and students having health and family problems.

5. Practice exercise creation: UTAs prepare students for papers with short homework assignments on which they provide immediate feedback.
6. Facilitation of team exercises in class: UTAs manage meetings of their teams when they are doing practice exercises.
7. Enforcement of rules: UTAs deduct points for students who are late, absent, asleep, or playing with their cell phones.
8. Recruitment of new UTAs for the next semester: A UTA is in charge of recruiting UTA applicants, scheduling applicant interviews, recording current UTA comments, and providing analysis to decide on the next semester's UTAs.
9. Research on data slides in class: UTAs get information to update slides.
10. Updating website content: A UTA provides updates to our webmaster in charge of the course.
11. Grading papers: UTAs double-grade papers using an elaborate rubric that runs 5–15 pages for each of the five course papers.
12. Reviewing the re-grade process: Several UTAs review requests for re-grades so students don't lose points they should not have lost.
13. Quality assurance: A UTA provides a review of the UTAs' behavior during each class and each meeting to improve team decision-making. They enforce classroom rules for UTAs by deducting points when a UTA misbehaves. If enough points are deducted, the UTA does not get an A in the course.
14. Office hours: Each of the 20 UTAs holds one weekly office hour so about 15 different office hours (some UTAs hold office hours at the same time) are offered to students.
15. Recruiting future students to the course: UTAs recruit their friends, whom they don't grade. The opportunity to become a UTA also helps recruit students to the course.

Grading student papers is the most difficult and controversial part of the use of UTAs at Syracuse. The majority of administrators and professors are horrified that undergraduates are grading undergraduates, and so are some undergraduates. Yet if you see students as developing professionals who are capable of doing the job, it should not be horrifying. If you see the course as one for developing skills, you will also see how students who also are developing skills can grade well.

What type of assignments you should allow UTAs to grade is an open question. Most professors would see no problem in UTAs grading multiple-choice tests using an answer key. Almost no professor would allow the grading of a research paper or test requiring answers of more than a paragraph. However, short-answer assignments can be graded if the rubrics are good enough.

One final point about grading by UTAs is that the grading requires attention to detail. This is a time-consuming and mundane task that a few professors would only do if, for example, there were 30 students and three two-page papers. UTAs at Syracuse use a system where every sentence is checked for grammar and typos and points are deducted for specified infractions. This allows grading of 900+ pages.

If you have enough UTAs so that no one will grade more than 10 papers at a time, it is possible to have short-answer papers or tests graded by UTAs. While the primary purpose of the UTA system is to provide the professor with vast resources to provide practice for students, the UTA experience itself is a powerful learning tool. They are in a complex organization where they have to manage their time to meet requirements. They practice all of the 38 skills in a situation where poor performance leads to bad consequences for both the course and them.

UTAs in large freshman classes also contribute to student engagement. The UTAs themselves are likely to be retained until graduation, creating a deeper connection to their university. The students will have a strong relationship with their UTA, which can make the difference between a student feeling isolated enough to transfer or knowing they have a person they can connect to.

The use of UTAs can be a primary source of happiness for you. They remove the routine work of grading for writing and following directions. They have taken the course and therefore are more expert than anyone else on what works and doesn't. They will be fixing small things that are important to the students in the class, like PowerPoints and handouts. However, they do add costs, such as for their own supervision and training. But everyone knows the road to happiness is one where benefits outweigh costs.

What: While you could incorporate the entire system of using UTAs described in this chapter, you may want to start small with one or two UTAs to add some components to the class, such as UTA office hours, creating a survey about outside speakers, grading selected papers, or reviewing lecture slides with you. You could make it an independent study where the UTA writes some kind of proposal to improve the course.

Materials Needed: Written guidelines on what the UTA is to do
Where: The classroom and in-office hours with the UTA
Skill Sets Practiced: All 10 skill sets

Chapter Eleven

Use Dale Carnegie Speeches

Don't criticize, condemn, or complain.

—Dale Carnegie

If this Carnegie quote were followed by everyone, it would lead not only to our personal happiness but also to a much better world. If you and your students practiced what Dale Carnegie preached, imagine how much more pleasant and productive your teaching would be.

Published in the 1930s, Dale Carnegie's *How to Win Friends and Influence People* has been translated into 55 languages, and it prompted the Dale Carnegie Institute, which conducts corporate and professional training. Give the book a quick read and decide if you want to assign it to your students. Even if you (or they) don't read the book, you can still make it a powerful force in your teaching. It is also an indirect way to provide diversity training without saying the *D* word.

What: Ask students to give the class a one-minute presentation organized into four sections in which they

1. state a personal problem they faced in anything they do (e.g., at home, school, the office),
2. state an action they took to correct the problem,
3. indicate the results of the action, and
4. cite the Carnegie principle used.

Have one Carnegie speech per class no matter what the size of the class. You can allow some discussion if you want, but the show-and-tell alone will build up trust in those principles over a few weeks.

Materials Needed: The Dale Carnegie List of Principles available at www.dalecarnegie.com; Dale Carnegie's *How to Win Friends and Influence People* (optional)

Where: The classroom

Skill Sets Practiced: Communicating Verbally; Working Directly with People; Influencing People; Solving Problems

Chapter Twelve

Create Groups for Small In-Class Assignments

> Before a group can enter the open society, it must close ranks.
> —Charles Vernon Hamilton

Two of the most powerful conditions motivating human behavior are the internal bonding within groups and competition when group members want to beat other groups. Using groupings in class can generate engagements among the students and more energy in class activities.

You can create groups in any size class as long as they are composed of at least four students. In a large class of 160 students, try 20 groups of eight. In a class of 15, three groups of five works. Use extra-credit points to motivate the groups to respond to questions, to draft example assignments, or to complete any activity that requires participation. Support within the group and a desire to beat other groups will get more hands raised than you expect.

To ensure that the groups bond within themselves, especially in large classes, you could ask each group to choose a name for themselves and to make a sign representing their group. Bring outside judges to choose the best name and sign, and you will have laid the seed of over-the-top engagement throughout the course.

In forming the groups, realize that the minimalist law prevails, so form the groups as you wish without overthinking it. Every process you choose has benefits and costs. You can do it randomly. You can also present a challenging topic to the class and form groups around their responses to make sure there is at least one member who has some clue and will be a strong student in the group. Much is published on this topic in the literature if you want enlightenment. Or just try something and see what happens.

The benefit of groups doing small exercises in class is more engagement within and outside the class. In addition, the group interactions are a constant source of entertainment and will give you something to observe psychologically. See how the groups interact and spot potential leaders for future work. The downside here is that you may have to listen to whining about other group members and the unfairness of the allocation of extra credit. You can turn this around and make the whining an upside by saying the process will prepare them for the teamwork and the unfairness that will be part of their lives.

What: During the first week or so, randomly assign students to groups. Have them sit together during the regular class periods and have places where the groups can spread out and meet. Create competition and motivation throughout the semester by allowing groups to earn extra-credit points.

Materials Needed: Create a PowerPoint for group point scores and update it every time points are handed out.

Where: The classroom

Skill Set Practiced: Working Directly with People

Chapter Thirteen

Set the Stage in the First Class

All the world's a stage.

—William Shakespeare

The first class will have a huge impact on student retention and performance so it is extremely important to build both trust and interest. The students are excited. They want to know what the deal is. They are judging your every move for trustworthiness.

As you are walking into the class, stop to talk to two students by introducing yourself and asking the students something about themselves. The other students will see this as evidence that you are a person and not just a professor.

Start the class with something memorable that shows that you are a caring person and that your course will mean something to the students. In addition, be clear on how the grading system will work. If the students believe you care, they will accept the grading system. Give them some information about yourself. To avoid them thinking you are arrogant (the normal reaction from someone who fears you because they think you have control over their life), you might say you are talking about yourself because the dean made you do it and you are a little embarrassed.

The goal here is to bring yourself to their level as someone helping, not force feeding, them.

You also need to do something out of the ordinary so they remember the class as something other than the grind they are about to face. You may want to show them your dog or your family or your hobby. Alternatively, you may want to create an event, like planting a student in the class who asks a question like why are the books so expensive?

For example, the author teaches a class in public policy and would ask the students, "What is a public policy?" At this point, he would tell the students to take out their wallets and locate an example. His shill in the audience would then say, "A driver's license." He would ask to see it then announce to the class it was clearly a fake ID. He would leave the room, then come back with scissors and cut the license in half. The student would rush out of the room while cussing him out. His students would have no trouble participating after that, eager to share their thoughts and opinions. He stopped doing this little act after a student's video of the class was picked up by Barstool and got millions of hits.

This was good because every student at Syracuse University knows about it but bad because the public relations team had a cow. Real TV covered it too, ending their 10-minute segment, "What This Professor Did," with "Oh, I see what the professor did; teach us a lesson on citizenship." Now the professor just shows students that segment instead of staging the act. It probably carries more weight than the event because today's students think if it is on TV, it's important. If my actions can cause such an uproar, imagine what an impact you could have as well.

Think of something dramatic to do that will give your students something to think about. You may question this type of event since students are to be treated as adults. Adults watching a play, act, or lecture like to be entertained so they'll feel less nervous about the new world they are entering. Since the principle of the individuality of the learner operates here, paying attention to getting buy-in is important. Being outside the box is the way to go in this day and age.

Students also want a clear syllabus handed out no later than the first class. Although they may be happy if you let them out early and don't conduct a formal class, you have let them down by keeping them in the dark. Always present material on the course the first day and make it clear what is in the syllabus. They will see it as a contract.

What: You know best how to brand yourself to your students during your first lecture. Be sure to follow Dale Carnegie's advice on relating to people. Have your books ordered (tell them how to get books cheaply) and use the first class for getting started on the material. They are watching you to learn how they can become good employees and good citizens.

Materials Needed: PowerPoints, a syllabus with a clear list of due dates, a video, maybe a planted shill doing some kind of skit

Where: The classroom

Skill Sets Practiced: Taking Responsibility; Asking and Answering the Right Questions

Chapter Fourteen

Use Simulations and Role Plays

> We are never more fully alive, more completely ourselves, or deeply engrossed in anything, than when we are at play.
> —Dr. Charles E. Schaefer, American psychologist

As an artist, you create experiences so students can practice skills while also possibly learning content. Think of role plays and simulations as painting a big picture on a blank canvas.

If you were to teach American government, for example, you could create a simulation where the students play members of the Constitutional Convention. You could ask students to play the role of current politicians and rewrite parts of the convention. Students would not have to read a textbook or listen to lectures about the convention; they would have to read the rules and learn the roles to play the game.

The primary goal of this and other simulations is learning content, not developing skills. Nevertheless, students practice many skills as an added bonus to becoming familiar with the content. Placing the content in a simulation format increases interest and participation. It also gives you a chance to think about the subject matter as you watch the students play the game. It will feed the artist in you.

What: Create a role-play or simulation exercise to illustrate the content of your course where the students play historical figures, people mentioned in the literature, or fictitious figures.

Materials Needed: A role-play or simulation exercise that requires rules, descriptions of the individuals to be played, and specific procedures to be followed

Where: The classroom for at least part of the activity, but the location could extend to activities taking place outside the classroom

Skill Sets Practiced: Communicating Verbally; Working Directly with People; Influencing People; Gathering Information; Asking and Answering the Right Questions; Solving Problems

Chapter Fifteen

Lie to the Class

> Believe nothing, no matter where you read it, or who said it, no matter if I have said it, unless it agrees with your own reason and your own common sense.
> —Buddha

The individuality of the learner requires that the student question everything to decide what they want to accept as truth. Among many things, this means treating their professor as another human being whose words have to make sense to them. One way to convey this early in the course is to intentionally say something in class that students should identify as false. Students who raise their hand and question the professor are practicing an important skill: Asking and Answering the Right Questions.

For example, if you are teaching history or political science, you could tell students that you saw an old copy of the Declaration of Independence when visiting Jefferson's house in Mount Vernon. You would hope more than one student would ask, "Didn't Jefferson live at Monticello?" or "Didn't George Washington live at Mount Vernon?" Respond by saying, "Yes, you are absolutely correct. I lied to see if anyone in the class actually knew the facts and also to warn you not to blindly accept everything I say. I make mistakes, and I also say things that are speculation that may or may not be true and may be interpreted differently."

This tactic has the added benefit of giving you a better perspective on the knowledge base of the class. It is an experiment that helps broaden your appreciation of what the students know and don't know. It also allows a discussion of how different backgrounds lead to differences in the knowledge base of students. Why should we expect students from different countries and backgrounds to know all the same facts?

In addition to developing the students' ability to always question everything, this serves to keep the professor from misleading students. For example, you may accidentally say an exercise is on page 10 when it is really on page 12. You want them to correct you and ignore the fear of being wrong or overstepping. It increases engagement and prevents you from having to make a retraction a day later. It also builds the relationship between you and the students as junior colleagues.

What: Early in the class, give some misinformation that the students should know is misinformation and praise the student that calls you out on it.

Materials Needed: None

Where: Usually the classroom, but you could try it in a private conversation with a student

Skill Sets Practiced: Asking and Answering the Right Questions; Solving Problems

Chapter Sixteen

Keep Your Mouth Shut

> I have always had a great respect for a Philippine proverb: "Into the closed mouth the fly does not get."
>
> —Theodore Roosevelt Jr.

Teaching is not telling. But professors were conditioned by talkers, so they typically talk *a lot*. There may be other factors operating in the inability of professors to shut up, like thinking all knowledge is equally important, needing attention, or constantly seeking new and bright members for their tribe. These pressures are difficult to avoid. Your UTAs will tell you this if you are fortunate and foresighted enough to have them. The key benefit of shutting up is that the classroom will be filled with the voices of the students rather than with your voice. This will promote more enthusiastic discussion and fewer blank stares. It will reduce the unpleasantness that silence from the class can create for you.

Like radio talk-show hosts, professors don't like "dead time" when students don't respond. You all have asked a question and gotten no answers. Studies have shown that faculty members rarely allow more than 5 seconds for a student to answer. If you allow 20 seconds, you will usually get a response. Class members don't like silence either, so someone will speak up.

When a class will not answer a question after prolonged prodding, tell them they have 30 seconds to talk with their neighbor and come up with an answer. This almost always works and actually does even more. In talking to their neighbor about the question, they are reviewing what has been said and exchanging ideas with each other.

Rephrasing your question may also work. It is better to say "What questions do you have?" than "Does anyone have any questions?" the latter of which is tantamount to merely asking about sheer understanding.

What: Carefully plan lectures to allow students to participate, and use the partner technique described above to get an answer. As one AA slogan suggests, always ask yourself, Why am I talking? (WAIT).

Materials Needed: Questions in PowerPoints that the class has to answer

Where: The classroom or anywhere you are talking to a student

Skill Sets Practiced: Communicating Verbally; Working Directly with People; Asking and Answering the Right Questions

Chapter Seventeen

Make Laptops and Smartphones Helpful

> Technology . . . the knack of so arranging the world that we don't have to experience it.
>
> —Homo Faber, Max Frisch character

Most professors find students' use of laptops and smartphones very annoying and a source of great unpleasantness. They take points off if they find a student using one for play. However, what if they call out a smartphone-using student only to find out the student was calculating quantitative information from the slide? What if the student has just found an error in the presentation?

On occasion, students sometimes use their laptops to fact check. The vice president of sustainability for United Technology was talking to a class at Syracuse University when a student went to an anti-business site and asked the speaker about something negative the site claimed about United Technology. The speaker was ready for the question and explained that the site was unreliable, but most of the students did not believe him.

Concern over the use of laptops and smartphones during class is reasonable. If you have a small class or a lot of UTAs to do the policing, you can deduct points if a student is caught using a laptop or smartphone to play. If not, there is not much you can do except live with it.

By encouraging students to use laptops and smartphones as part of the class activity, you will enhance the quality of the discussion and the engagement of the students. In addition, you may decide to have students answer closed-choice questions on their smartphones and then display the results on the screen to enhance discussions.

Rather than seeing laptops and smartphones as a source of disengagement, you can generate engagement by making laptops and smartphones part of the class. In doing so, you will generate engagement and much happiness for yourself.

What: Announce in class that laptops and smartphones can be used to add to whatever is being discussed. You might want to give extra points for perceptive and useful remarks.

Materials Needed: None, except perhaps a note in the syllabus and a slide in any early class when discussing the use of laptops and smartphones

Where: The classroom as well as in workshop-type meetings

Skill Set Practiced: Asking and Answering the Right Questions

Part IV

Organizational Tactics

The chapters in this section will help you develop your syllabus and run activities within your class. They cover a wide variety of tactics. Some of these tactics, like those in the next three chapters, may require a major change in your teaching, while others may align more with what you do already. These tactics are a logical outcome of the roles and strategies discussed in the previous sections.

Chapter Eighteen

Start with the Concrete and Familiar

Don't bite off more than you can chew.

—Anonymous

One of the biggest mistakes most professors make is to start with the general and stay with it too long. For example, they may try to explain the federal system of government in the United States. This usually results in students memorizing the definition but being unable to apply that definition in a meaningful way. Many professors, regardless of academic field, make the mistake of starting and staying too general without concrete examples, especially in introductory courses.

The best way to start the discussion of an abstract term, like "federalism," is to not mention the term initially. Instead, provide an example, like standardized testing, that students are all familiar with. Explain that the local school board has been forced to implement standardized testing because the state government requires it and the federal government encourages it through funding and requirements. Then spring the word "federalism" on them and explain that sharing power or fighting over power among the levels of government is what the term means. A discussion can then follow in which students can assess the benefits and costs of federalism in education based on their personal experience and knowledge.

The importance of starting with concrete and familiar examples may be viewed as a form of scaffolding. Educational professionals know the important of scaffolding in K–12 education, but college professors tend to be maximalists and want to get to a high level as quickly as possible. If you can provide a concrete example that students understand, you will then be able to build your learners' understanding of the subject by providing more examples that they might not be familiar with.

Once concrete examples are adequately described, you can then provide general or theoretical ideas. The federalist discussion presented would work in the field of policy. A similar approach could be used in other fields. In science, labs are places where students can become familiar with abstract concepts through concrete examples—that is, by conducting experiments. In the humanities, an easily accessible piece of literature could serve a similar purpose.

Starting a new subject by talking about the general will lead most students to memorize words and never understand them. Professors love abstraction; most students, not so much.

What: Prepare examples and stories that the student is likely to find familiar and suggest how they reflect the general idea. If relevant, prompt students to talk about their personal experiences.

Materials Needed: A reading, video, or story that students are likely to understand from their own experiences

Where: The classroom or anywhere you might use a concrete and familiar example to help your students grasp an abstract concept

Skill Set Practiced: Asking and Answering the Right Questions

Chapter Nineteen

Use Modules

Break big tasks into smaller pieces to avoid distractions.

—Eric Ravenscraft

The idea of three-credit or four-credit courses may appear to make sense because it is the current norm for most colleges. The 45 hours of instruction put together with readings, lectures, and other activities and assignments or tests is arbitrary. The three- or four-credit course is not going to change, but it is better to design courses to identify "modules," or relatively compact units, and string them together.

About 40 years ago, curriculum developers started using the term "modules," which can be thought of as "learning chunks" that can stand alone or be used in a class with other pieces. Although it is sometimes best to resist curriculum specialist-speak, thinking in terms of modules will help you focus sections on a specific learning objective. The material within each module is focused on a single overall objective, but taken together, the entire course becomes coherent.

You may want to use the term "modules" instead of "papers" or "term papers." It will help your students see there are separate clusters of learning outcomes for different but linked components of the course. The term itself takes on a branding function.

Think of course design as creating a set of learning activities that might stand alone and be loosely connected to the overall theme. You will then be focused on connecting your educational goals to the activities more clearly, and your students will see a beginning and an end.

There is another advantage to modules if you are part of a team creating an interdisciplinary course. You and your colleagues can work on each part separately rather than getting mired in the big picture. Agreement and division of labor are then easier to reach and implement.

What: Identify and create self-contained modules in your class and work to get class activities focused on each module's learning objective.

Materials Needed: The usual materials from readings plus assignments

Where: The classroom and in online courses

Skill Sets Practiced: Any of the 10 skill sets, depending on the topic and activities

Chapter Twenty

Use Class Time for Coaching

> The least of the work of learning is done in the classroom.
> —Thomas Merton

Take a leaf from the teaching of art and architecture, where much of the scheduled class time consists of students working on projects or assignments. Science labs, too, are workshops where assistants help students conduct experiments. You can do this for any subject matter.

If you use all of your class time to lecture and discuss, you are missing the opportunity of working as a coach for your students, and your students are missing enriching practice time. A significant attribute of a class meeting is that students and the professor are in close proximity. It is a mistake to only use one physical configuration: facing the student and talking. If you adopt a coaching framework, you can view what your students are doing and offer help. This is necessary for group projects as well as individual work. Consider changing from a lecturing to a workshop format. You can then provide direct help to students who need your advice, and at the same time, for example, a student will be able to ask whoever is sitting next to them for help.

A workshop format shifts the dynamic of the class meeting away from the professor talking or leading a discussion, allowing space for the individuality of the learner. Students will see it as a gift from you so they can get their assignments done efficiently. As a general rule, people who receive gifts are nice to the gift-giver. Students who provide genuine appreciation give professors joy.

What: View some class periods as workshop time to get things done. You can act as a group and individual coach.

Materials Needed: Data; assignments; project directions; templates; relevant research or scholarly literature

Where: The classroom

Skill Sets Practiced: Communicating Verbally; Gathering Information; Using Quantitative Tools; Asking and Answering the Right Questions; Solving Problems

Chapter Twenty-One

Debriefing Competitions

> The way to get things done is to stimulate competition. I do not mean in a sordid, money-getting way, but in the desire to excel.
>
> —Charles Schwab

Most faculty members start teaching skills or content with readings and lectures. They may also do some demonstrations or case studies in class. There is nothing wrong with this approach, but it is usually not enough.

At some point, try the tactic of having the class, either individually or in groups, discover what is wrong with a sample assignment of what they will be submitting soon. Depending on the size of the assignment and the number of students in the class, this "debriefing competition" can take 1–3 classes.

Students can meet in groups to do the sample assignment. This sample assignment is similar to the individual assignment they will complete for the course, but it is on a different topic. During the next class or two, put up one of their products (or have a canned one just to make it easier) and call on groups to identify an error in the material presented. If a group identifies an error correctly, all the members of the group receive an extra-credit point or two. If they get it wrong, call on another group and continue to do so until all the errors have been found. Don't punish wrong answers because then students will be afraid to answer.

The promise of extra credit provides strong motivation. This is not just because the members of each group want to have their grade increased but also because they want to beat the other groups. Also, people in the group who usually don't participate may pitch in. When asked what was most helpful in doing well on a paper, most students cite this debriefing competition. You can use this competitive debriefing tool for any paper or test preparation. It is more fun for the students and you than a traditional review session. The debriefing of a sample assignment beats the traditional way of preparing students for a written assignment. The traditional procedure ignores the fact that each student has a different perspective and is at a different stage of writing the assignment.

What: Provide students with an incorrect sample of a written assignment and allow them to identify errors in it. You can do debriefings during class time without using groups or without using extra credit, but using both will increase engagement. In addition, you could have students complete another exercise to prepare for the debriefing. It is best to use this procedure about two days before the assignment is due since most students will not have started it earlier.

Materials Needed: Samples of written work you assign
Where: The classroom
Skill Sets Practiced: All 10 skill sets

Chapter Twenty-Two

Create Lateness and Absence Policies

Procrastination is the art of keeping up with yesterday.

—Don Marquis

Helping students develop their time management skills is essential to preparing them to have successful careers and be responsible citizens. If you include in your job description preparing students to do well and do good, you need to include in every course you teach a learning objective called Time Management. You don't want one of your students to inform his boss one day that he could not attend a staff meeting because he had scheduled a tennis date for that time. The media and pundits like to blame this kind of outrageous behavior on whatever "generation" an individual is from. Professors who don't hold students responsible for getting work done on time need to share the blame.

While there are plenty of legitimate excuses for lateness and absence, you need to establish clear guidelines and sanctions. Without them, you will be forced to make too many ad hoc decisions. You will also be sending a signal that irresponsible behavior is okay.

You may want to develop some rules for unexcused lateness—beyond a few minutes—or absence from class. One idea is that students lose points. Requests for excused absences or lateness are reviewed on an ad hoc basis if made prior to an infraction.

Or you could do what one professor at Syracuse University does: He locks the door to the classroom when class starts. This "nuclear" option seems to work.

Many professors do not see class attendance as mandatory. They don't have an explicit set of punishments. However, they make a mental note of a student's lack of attendance or lateness and take it out on the student in some way. This passive-aggressive behavior by professors has to be viewed as a sign of unhappiness. Just as corporations see attendance at mid-career training as mandatory, the practice for college teaching should be the same. You should have very clear policies for handing in assignments on time, and they should be described in the syllabus and mentioned during the first day of class. Students need structure, and you will be happier with a strong system of rules in place.

What: Establish clear rules for unexcused absence from class or lateness

Materials Needed: A syllabus that clearly outlines your unexcused lateness and absence policies

Where: Your syllabus and the classroom

Skill Set Practiced: Taking Responsibility

Chapter Twenty-Three

Distinguish Between Points Earned and Points Lost

Life is an aggregation problem.

—Bill Coplin

The tactic described in this chapter applies to written assignments, whether in-class written examinations or take-home papers. The tactic does not apply to multiple-choice tests where students earn points for the right answers.

It is best to have two sets of criteria to determine student grades for written assignments. The first results in earning points and the second results in losing points. The former acts as an incentive for doing what is assigned and the latter as a penalty for doing something wrong other than having an incorrect answer. This includes writing mistakes, lateness in submitting papers, using the wrong format, and not following directions.

By separating content mistakes, you help the student focus on what needs to be corrected. If you lump these points in with the determination of total points available, students will be not clear on where they went wrong. This distinction helps students figure out what is caused by carelessness, poor attention to detail, or time management versus what is caused by a lack of understanding of the material or failure to answer the question asked.

This is especially true with respect to writing. Just as war is too important to leave to the generals, as French statesman Georges Clemenceau said after World War I, writing is way too important to leave to the writing instructors. This is the case because writing improves with practice and a freshman writing course does not give enough practice because it is often limited to one semester. With the advent of texting, social media, and email, writing is worse than it has ever been for students entering the real world.

These two types of grades will make your life easier and therefore happier.

What: A grading breakdown into points earned for providing the correct answer and points lost for such things as lateness, writing mistakes, and various forms of poor organization

Materials Needed: Clear and explicit information in the syllabus on how points determining grades can be won or lost

Where: Your grade sheets

Skill Sets Practiced: Taking Responsibility; Solving Problems; Using Quantitative Tools

Chapter Twenty-Four

Use Extra-Credit Points to Stimulate Extra Practice

> Education should learn from the positive side of gaming—reward, accomplishment, and fun.
>
> —Sebastian Thrun

Use extra-credit points to encourage students to do things like attend a lecture or complete community-service hours. Provide incentives so students get experiences outside the classroom that will benefit those who are interested. Every field has applications that could justify rewarding points.

You may want to consider some of these outside experiences as course requirements rather than extra credit. However, this may result in creating more work for you, which as a minimalist is the opposite of what a happy professor should do. It might make more sense to open the opportunity but not mandate it.

The students' motivation to go to extra-credit opportunities is the desire for higher grades. There is no way to get around this, but those extra-credit opportunities may engage the students, especially if they are not doing as well as they want in the class.

Another benefit to extra credit is that you can grade more stringently without giving too many Ds and Fs in the course. Students lose many writing and organizational points despite having okay content. Extra-credit opportunities will enable you to get students to pay attention to detail but not make it the primary cause of low grades and dropped courses. Giving students second chances that lead to improvement is a key to happiness in dealing with students having difficulties in a course. Extra-credit opportunities are that second chance.

What: Extra-credit opportunities for students to learn through direct observation or participation outside the classroom

Materials Needed: Information on your syllabus on how to obtain the extra-credit points and slides highlighting why outside experiences are important

Where: The classroom

Skill Sets Practiced: All 10 skill sets

Chapter Twenty-Five

Use Group Presentations as Teamwork Practice

> The strength of the team is each individual member. The strength of each member is the team.
>
> —Phil Jackson

Most faculty members rightly see group presentations to the class or people outside the class as a way to improve presentation skills. However, these presentations can be used for much more, especially practicing teamwork. The process leading up to and following the presentations will help students practice most of the 10 skill sets.

The reason presentations are such a powerful learning experience is that students worry what their audience will think about them. While students might use some time in writing a paper worth 30% of their grade, they will spend much more time in preparing for a presentation worth 10% of their grade. In assigning a presentation to students, you are unleashing energy that is not always there for other assignments. This is especially true for group presentations.

In addition, individual and group presentations promote student engagement. They have no alternative but to participate—if only to get a good grade. This forced participation can, many times, change a student's role in the course from passive to active, and with long-term implications.

Many faculty members require dress rehearsals and coach students on their PowerPoints, their verbal performance, and their timing. Others just let the students do what they want to do with no rehearsing or coaching. As long as you decide on the goals of the presentation in terms of skill development and content mastery and allocate the time accordingly, how much coaching you want to do is your choice. Some professors might want to "make sure" that the presentation is of high quality because they feel it reflects on them. Trying to make sure a student presentation will be of high quality is a violation of minimalist principles. It is legitimate to worry about the quality of a final presentation, but remember the laws of the minimalist and the validity of the idea that the best learning is from mistakes. A faculty member spending an inordinate amount of time helping fine-tune a final presentation may lead to a better presentation, but it is not clear that the student will do a better job in the future. Perhaps making mistakes on their own will better prepare them. True education is always about the future. The present can only be practice for the student.

A key factor students should consider is the purpose of the presentation. Is it to describe an existing condition or problem, to raise awareness and convince their audience something is important, or to present some kind of planned action in a descriptive or argumentative way? To put it more simply, is it about facts or an attitude adjustment? You can prescribe the purpose of the presentation or you can let the students decide, as long as they can tell you at the beginning or end of the presentation what they are trying to do.

Some very simple, mechanical rules should be emphasized. First, students should always figure out how to look forward and never turn their back on the audience to look at the screen. Second, students should never go beyond the time allotted. Cut them off if they do, even if it is in the middle of a sentence. Third, students should connect with their audience in some way. Fourth, students should welcome questions and comments at the end of the talk unless these are permitted during the talk. Finally, the fewer words and fancy things on a slide, the better.

What: Incorporate individual or group presentations in the course. For smaller classes, a formal presentation could be required. For all classes, you might require a brief talk of one minute, or you can coach during a normal exchange among the students.

Materials Needed: For formal presentations, the one-page rubric you will use in evaluating the presentations

Where: The classroom

Skill Sets Practiced: Most of the 10 skill sets, especially Communicating Verbally

Part V

Remedial Tactics

You may not want to accept the role of helping students catch up on basic skill development, but even your "best" students may lack some of the skills discussed in this section. Complaining about poor high school preparation is not useful unless you do something about it. This section provides tactics designed to help students perform the tasks you would like them to perform. They will not require much time or work on your part, but they could make a big difference.

Chapter Twenty-Six

Writing to Communicate

> It is a good thing for an uneducated man to read books of quotations.
> —Winston Churchill

In most cases, students' ability to write for the purpose of communicating information is poor. There are many reasons for this, including an emphasis in writing classes on writing to express emotion or to argue an idea. Moreover, grammatical rules are not practiced consistently throughout the education of most students.

No matter what the reason, every professor should be a writing coach by rewarding clear and brief writing and punishing unclear and disorganized writing. In some fields, writing to express emotion or argue for an idea may be a reasonable goal, but in all fields the ability to communicate clearly through writing will benefit students in life after college.

Helping students improve their written communication is no small task. You face a broad range of different writing problems, including students who speak English as a second language or students who have been led by previous teachers to believe that writing must entertain the reader or that "the more words the better." Most have had little or no training in grammar. To help students communicate better through writing, you must work one-on-one and grade in detail.

Writing is way too important to be confined to a freshman writing course. Writing instructors generally do what they can; however, writing improves with practice, and a freshman writing course does not give enough practice. With the advent of texting, social media, and email, students' writing is worse than it has ever been.

The best way to improve the writing of your students is to use, on a few occasions, short-answer assignments of fewer than 200 words. A clear rubric for content can be easily developed so you can concentrate on things like punctuation and citation form.

Long essays and papers are not as good a vehicle for helping students with grammar and written communication. Today, with the use of computers and online courses and surveys, short answers have become the norm. This tactic not only makes it easier to identify and correct writing problems, it also prepares students for what they will face in their careers and as citizens.

Unfortunately, the training in writing that undergraduates receive suffers from a lack of consistent practice and direct coaching in the form of corrections. It also suffers from the tendency of professors to reward bulk. Most professors want their students to write as if they were participating in scholarly activities. Only the members of a scholarly tribe want to read the specialized language of that tribe. To most outside the tribe, their writing is incomprehensible.

What: Grade all written work for grammar and spelling. Use the system described in chapter 23 by deducting points separately for writing mistakes and for content mistakes.

Materials Needed: Short-answer assignments of fewer than 200 words with a clear rubric for content

Where: Inside and outside the classroom

Skill Set Practiced: Communicating in Writing

Chapter Twenty-Seven

Improve Typing

The only thing I learned in high school was how to type.

—Anonymous

Today, students may or may not have practiced typing. Those who haven't practiced type slower and make more mistakes than those who have a sustained practice experience.

Typing class is different from most other classes in high school. The teacher leaves the student alone and never says much more than "Do typing exercise three." Success in typing class is not based on a teacher's evaluation. Typing is practicing a skill with a defined system of measurement that determines the student's skill level.

You may reject the suggestion that you should do something about your undergraduates' typing skills. No professor would consider it to be in their job description or in their learning outcomes, but by doing so you can help make a major improvement in the lives of many undergraduates, especially those with poor high school preparation. And, most importantly, you can do it in five minutes of class time.

If you are wondering why this five minutes is necessary, you only have to watch students typing today. They may be good with two thumbs on their smartphones, but how many can type at least 40 words per minute adjusted for typos? K–12 education may have keyboarding classes, but many give little or no attention to the practice necessary to build typing skills.

Good typing skills are a key to a successful career. Students can be the typist for team projects in some cases and become the de facto leader of the team. De facto leaders become official leaders. Good typists can also perform data entry more quickly and accurately than those who can't match their performance. This can lead to staffing jobs to generate income and pay the bills until they get a permanent job . . . and it can even lead to a permanent job.

Students can improve their typing skills through free online programs, but you may need to incentivize them. You can give extra credit to students who reach a certain word-per-minute rate or who attend makeshift workshops you create. These steps will replace something missing from their K–12 education and greatly improve their efficiency in completing written assignments.

What: Typing practice

Materials Needed: A typing tutoring program like TypingCat (https://thetypingcat.com) may be a good place to start.

Where: Outside the classroom

Skill Sets Practiced: Taking Responsibility; Developing Physical Skills

Chapter Twenty-Eight

Simple Computer Applications

> Computers are like Old Testament gods: lots of rules and no mercy.
> —Joseph Campbell, *The Power of Myth*

Just as you cannot assume all of your students in a given class have the same content background, you cannot assume they all have basic computer skills. Your goal should be to bring all students in the class up to a basic level of use in Microsoft Office applications. If they have a Mac laptop, your college should be able to give them a free version of Office for Mac. You also need to make sure that they can access and use whatever electronic material is used in the class, including Blackboard, Google Docs, and any websites. Students should also be able to use email and have access to it. Many students may have inadequate computers and not know where to find university-based facilities. Make that information available.

The law of the minimalist applies here. Here is a brief list of necessary skills in Microsoft Office:

Word

- Create a document
- Save a document
- Use spelling and grammar check
- Insert page numbers
- Track changes
- Cut and paste text

PowerPoint

- Create a slideshow
- Add slides
- Add titles to slides

Excel

- Create a spreadsheet
- Create a simple graph
- Create a simple table

Hopefully most of your students are able to do these functions, but some may not. You don't want students doing poorly in the class because they have trouble accessing and using basic computer software.

What: A way to identify students who lack basic computer skills and help them get those skills. You could give a simple diagnostic test at the beginning of class and ask savvier classmates to help their fellow students develop these minimal skills. It is not suggested that you send them to a training workshop because these workshops usually try to cover too much. A buddy system always works better.

Materials Needed: A diagnostic test and a list of remedial resources

Where: Inside and outside the classroom

Skill Sets Practiced: Communicating in Writing; Using Quantitative Tools

Chapter Twenty-Nine

Excel Is Life

> Finance Pros Say You'll Have to Pry Excel Out of Their Cold, Dead Hands
> —*Wall Street Journal* headline

Students are greatly disadvantaged in college and in the workforce if they have little or no experience with Excel. They will have trouble getting internships. Even if they do get one, they won't be able to help their supervisors as much as they should. And then, when they look for a job? Most employers will require evidence of competence in Excel.

Our K–12 system rarely ensures mastery of Excel. Some students may have had a class or a section of a class that introduced them to Excel sometime between the sixth and twelfth grade, but many students will have not. One class is rarely enough for students to be strong enough to offer it to potential employers anyway.

College students are more likely than high school graduates to get Excel practice in their coursework. However, many college students get through college without practicing Excel. If only struggling art majors with dreams of being a professional artist knew that Excel could help them achieve their goals, they wouldn't be starving artists for long. While pursuing their dreams, they could work for a staffing firm for $25.00 an hour. When they need to take inventory of their paintings, market their product, and maintain a record of profit and losses, they can use Excel to be successful. Since they love art, they will have a better chance of getting a job as a museum administrator if Excel is under their belt.

Watch out for courses and experiences that try to get students to master statistical packages that are useful primarily for academic researchers. These packages are okay for some students who are moving in that direction, but the vast majority only need to be experienced with Excel. And while you're at it, watch out for some of the newer programs that provide enhanced visualization. They are used by consulting firms but not by the vast majority of business, government, and nonprofit organizations. Do your students a favor and remind them: Excel is life.

What: An ability to use Microsoft Excel. Give your students some raw data and have them create a spreadsheet and a brief, descriptive report of a finding. That will get them started. If you want one example, see the assignment in chapter 31.

Materials Needed: Raw data, a computer, and Microsoft Excel
Where: Anywhere
Skill Set Practiced: Using Quantitative Tools

Chapter Thirty

Information Searching Basics

> Without Google, Wikipedia, Chrome and other search engines, everybody would be greatly less informed in just about every area of knowledge.
> —Atam Ayomanor

Students today face good news and bad news. The good news is that they can access unlimited information through their computers. The bad news is they frequently can't find the useful and credible information they really need. You can help your students by giving assignments that force them to practice the art of information searching.

Faculty members frequently complain that students don't know much. You can blame the lack of knowledge on the education system or social media all you want, but the massive increase in available information and the increasing complexity and interdependence of the world limits the capacity of students to store data in their brains and access it quickly.

As we cannot increase their capacity to store data in their heads, there is no alternative but to help students practice information searches. One way to promote practicing information searching is to use the idea discussed in chapter 17 of encouraging students to use their laptops and smartphones to search for information pertinent to what you are saying in class. If you get students in the habit, this fact checking will help improve their information searching skills.

One of the biggest difficulties is how to get students started on an information search. If you don't give them a specific term to begin the search or the term is too general, they will have difficulty doing a search. They may be interested in researching crime but may be unable to figure out what specific topic within that general topic they want to study. Give them some ideas. Students can visit the library and find a book, or they can Google the term and get thousands of related topics. You may want to suggest that students start off by looking at Wikipedia, which has broad and historical descriptions of many subjects as well as many citations that students may want to further examine. Although Wikipedia is viewed as unreliable by many because of its crowdsourcing format, some now consider it to be as reliable as other basic sources of information like encyclopedias for introductory purposes.

What: Introduce students to commercial databases, like ProQuest, by having them use a relevant database to find something about a topic that interests them. Those who say students require some background to find a publication relevant to what they are studying frequently criticize this scavenger-hunt approach. But how do students get started if they know nothing?

The scavenger-hunt approach gets the student to use existing tools even if the practice leads to nothing useful. The searching and finding process itself will begin to inform the student. Grade the assignment on whether or not they found something rather than on the quality of what they found.

Materials Needed: Commercial databases and an assignment to find information relevant to the topic you have assigned

Where: The classroom and online

Skill Sets Practiced: Gathering Information; Asking and Answering the Right Questions

Chapter Thirty-One

Survey Basics Required

> Everyone takes surveys. Whoever makes a statement about human behavior has engaged in a survey of some sort.
>
> —Andrew Greerly

Surveys are everywhere, shaping the policies of business, informing nonprofits and government, and contributing largely to media coverage of politics. Familiarity with designing, conducting, and analyzing survey results is important for everyone's career and increasingly important for being an active and effective citizen.

As consumers of survey results, students need to understand the many factors that limit the usefulness of survey results. Questions about the sample used in a survey and how representative the sample of the target population always needs to be asked so that the student understands sampling bias. The wording of questions and the way surveys are conducted can generate findings that may not reflect what they are supposed to. Deciding on whom to vote for and understanding the impact of existing policies are shaped by survey results despite lousy samples and the poor or leading questions in most surveys reported in the media.

Students need to know how their survey results could be questionable, like if the survey is not representative by being from only one group or if it's not accurate because the respondents felt pressure to answer one way or another. Let your students know that the results are always biased by the people paying for or conducting the survey and that the results are always speculative. If they are armed with this information, they are better equipped to make surveys that may be useful.

What: You may not be teaching a subject that is traditionally studied through surveys, but they can be used in every class. Distribute a paper survey the first day of class that includes no more than five questions. Two questions should be demographic, like the student's major or year. Three questions should be about the student's class expectations (or anything attitudinal like that). Tell your students to use Excel and present the findings for each of the five questions. Then have the class critique the presentations.

During the process, you will have concrete tasks to coach: question making, determining representativeness, determining accuracy, etc. You will need to provide specific guidelines for the process. You can use this exercise in any subject area, not just the social sciences, by having a few questions about the subject matter of the course. This activity will also serve to promote some class bonding. If you have groups, try to have each group include one student with experience in quantitative analysis.

Materials Needed: A paper survey distributed on the first day of class
Where: The classroom
Skill Sets Practiced: Gathering Information; Using Quantitative Tools

Chapter Thirty-Two

Quantitative Tools Are Not About Mathematics

It is the mark of a truly intelligent person to be moved by statistics.
—George Bernard Shaw

Quantitative analysis is the use of mathematical tools in an applied way. It requires practice of the basics and the use, but not calculation, of statistics. The focus should always be on whether your students can perform the important initial tasks. Unfortunately, many professors move on to quantitative techniques that are more advanced than they should be before the students have mastered the basics. This results in the poor use of numbers by students, not to mention widespread fear and anxiety that prevents students from getting the skills they need as employees and citizens.

The laws of the minimalist are very important in preparing students for the use of quantitative tools. What they are taught in statistics classes often goes too deep, trying to get students to understand the formulas and covering too many types of statistics rather than having them practice applications. As a result, many students come into a junior-level research methods course unable to

- use percentages
- apply the difference between an absolute number and a percentage or rate
- create a spreadsheet and codebook in Excel
- distinguish and apply the difference between nominal and ordinal or interval data
- organize and display raw numbers for analysis
- distinguish between the representativeness and the accuracy of data

Reducing anxiety around numbers and math is one of the most important things you can do for your students with respect to both personal problems, careers, and citizenship. In some cases, it is like giving a blind person sight. Since female students suffer from number anxiety more than male students, you will also be striking a blow for gender equality.

What: Give your students quantitative data in your lectures and exercises where they do simple things like compare rates and percentages or compare demographic variables across different countries. Bar and trend line graphs should be used the most in lectures, and assignments with the occasional use of contingency tables can be used once students master with plenty of practice univariate analysis.

Materials Needed: A dataset or a simple survey you have created related to the content of your course. Use simple graphs and tables in your lectures and assignments.

Where: The classroom

Skill Sets Practiced: Using Quantitative Tools; Gathering Information

Part VI

Citizenship Tactics

This section provides ideas on how to help students become better citizens by acquiring the basic skills and general perspectives most necessary for the responsible exercise of citizenship.

The tactics in this section, while useful for careers, are essential for adults who will behave as responsible citizens. Most educators who claim to help students become better citizens believe that it can be done through readings that range from America's founding fathers to Saul Alinsky. As we have found obvious over the years, good thinking and content mastery of whatever subject, including the social sciences, does not a good citizen make. Only experience and the character of the student does.

Chapter Thirty-Three

The Easy Way to Community Engagement

Involve me and I learn.

—Benjamin Franklin

Many of the tactics and strategies suggested throughout this book require experiences both within and outside the university. Those experiences outside the university are part of the increasing role universities play in improving the communities in which they are located. This is a key way in which to build both skills and realistic attitudes among students so they can be helpful citizens.

Community engagement can be practiced by every undergraduate program in the university, not just those in the social sciences and professional schools.

Students in fields like the social sciences could help people in the community learn to use the tools and techniques of their fields. Those in the physical sciences and humanities could serve as tutors to K–12 students or could put on classroom demonstrations. It is not just what the students bring to the community, but what the community brings to the students.

Be pragmatic in involving your students. You have students who want to improve their community and who have valuable skills and knowledge to help government and nonprofit agencies. Whether it is an after-school program, a project like apple picking, or administrative work like data analysis or fundraising, all are worthwhile endeavors.

Some faculty say that students might go to a community center and be given nothing to do. They might just talk to their friends or play with their smartphones. Don't worry that some students might not engage. The student will learn through experience that passivity just doesn't work in today's world. They might refuse to engage the first time, but they will be better prepared when faced with another new situation. If you are worried that they will be earning a grade that they do not deserve, just relax on this one. Sitting around a place like a bump on a log is punishment enough.

What: In class, survey students to learn what skills and past experiences they have. Have your students generate a list of nonprofits that will be offered students to perform a variety of tasks, like tutoring and mentoring. Create a simple flyer that offers help in those areas and email it to the directors of the nonprofits with a contact number that might be yours, your graduate assistant's, or that of a student in the class. Have your students contact the agency and set up a time to meet to write a contract and then have them send you the contract. Give extra credit or make it a requirement in the course. Basically, you are setting up your own staffing firm. After one or two pilot efforts, you will have a community engagement machine that runs itself.

My program provides more than 20,000 hours of volunteer services and more than 60 projects that are highly valued by their organizations. These include conducting and designing surveys, doing research for annual reports and grants, and providing database assistance. My community partners say the value of these services is more than $100,000 each year.

Materials Needed: A list of local nonprofit and community agencies offering free services

Where: The classroom and your community

Skill Sets Practiced: Taking Responsibility; Communicating Verbally; Working Directly with People; Influencing People; Asking and Answering the Right Questions; Solving Problems

Chapter Thirty-Four

Use Continuums to Avoid the Role of Propagandist

> Do not expect to arrive at certainty in every subject which you pursue. There are a hundred things wherein we mortals . . . must be content with probability, where our best light and reasoning will reach no farther.
> —Isaac Watts

Working with students on controversial subjects like climate change, poverty, the criminal justice system, evolution, and topics like abortion or racism can lead to unhappiness and stress. Professors feel constrained and worried that what they say may be viewed as offensive. The best way to avoid feeling this way is to use continuums when discussing these topics.

Whatever your political beliefs, never view your students as recruits. It can only lead to hard feelings and unhappiness for both your students and yourself.

If you have a burning desire to tell students you are a Marxist or a member of some political party, tell them. If you do so to convert, you violate the integrity of what an academic should be. You will be unhappy if you fail to convert. If you are successful, you will increase pressure on yourself to convert more. Over the long run, it can only lead to unhappiness for the majority of your students and some of your colleagues.

It is preferable not to tell students your beliefs because no matter what you say or do, many students will think they have to support your views or that their grades are low because you disagree with them. If you are running small discussion classes, the ideological majority will attack the ideological minority, which will make your job of maintaining neutrality difficult. If you have a clearly stated position, whatever you say will be viewed as coercive.

The reason students will feel that they have to agree with you is inherent in the existing power relationship between you as the authority and the student as the repository of your views. If you thoroughly embrace the idea of the individuality of the learner and your students believe it, you may have a chance they will be honest with you. Otherwise, their focus on grades as the most important takeaway from your course will lead to suspicion and unhappiness for both of you.

You should help students explore topics with an open mind. One of the important results of an undergraduate education as well as career and citizenship success is the ability to think independently. The happy professor doesn't teach students what to think but rather helps them acquire the ability to think for themselves. They should learn to seek more information from more viewpoints.

Using continuums is a form of the traditional pro and con expressed on a two-pole spectrum. This allows for more than a binary choice and emphasizes that things can easily change by moving along the continuum. The use of a continuum also changes the discussion from an "argument" over who is right to a discussion of where others are on the continuum and where the student is on the continuum at the time of the discussion.

The purpose of an argument is to convince the other person you are right. This may be fun and inherent in the human condition, but it should not be the staple of an education. The use of continuums forces a consideration that black-and-white has to give way to gray.

These continuums should be used for different content in the course. After a few applications, students will get used to the idea of thinking about two poles and the space between them. It admittedly oversimplifies because in the real world things are rarely dichotomous, but it follows the law of the minimalist. Get them to think in terms of dichotomies so they can eventually think in terms of multiples.

What: Continuums can be used as a framework for class discussion or written assignments. In the list below, examples are divided into three types of discussions: value conflicts, explanations, and predictions. There can be overlap among the three.

Value Conflicts (Where Are You?)

Doing well—Doing good
Freedom—Order
Status quo—Change
Anti-abortion—Abortion
Idealist—Realist
Self-interest—Public interest

Explanations (Why Something Happens)

Nature—Nurture
People are basically good—People are basically bad
Poverty is caused by a lack of responsibility—The system
Bart Simpson—Bill Gates
Globalism—Nationalism

Predictions

What will not happen—What will happen
Consequences will be bad—Consequences will be good
Intended—Unintended
Benefits—Costs

Materials Needed: One of these lists incorporated in a lecture or used as a prompt for a paper or any written assignment. Use a continuum as a figure on a PowerPoint for class discussion or in the assignment.

Where: The classroom or in written assignments

Skill Sets Practiced: Asking and Answering the Right Questions; Solving Problems

Chapter Thirty-Five

Use Problem-Solving Exercises

A problem well stated is a problem half solved.

—Charles F. Kettering

In every field, there are undesirable conditions that need to be ameliorated. These are not mathematical or logic-based problems where there is a known solution. In the real world, there are no permanent solutions—only steps to improve things. However, as a matter of shorthand, the word "problem-solving" is used in this discussion of helping students apply a problem-solving model. This model is something they will have to use in their personal lives, their careers, and their civic activities.

The most important component of a problem-solving model is identifying a problem. Whether as an individual or group, we have a natural tendency to start with solutions rather than with a clear definition of the problem and a clear understanding of the likely causes of the problem. We typically jump to conclusions about what needs to be done.

For example, the board of a senior citizens organization might conclude that their weekly lunches are not well attended but then argue over how to improve publicity to attract participants. They might then debate many actions to improve publicity rather than first look at the information they have about the lunches, including attendance patterns and comments by attendants. Perhaps, for example, the lunches are not appetizing or are held on the wrong day.

Frequently, board meetings and faculty meetings do not seek a clear definition of a problem or any data from research on factors leading to the problem before discussing solutions. Sometimes those attending don't want to be "negative" so they may even avoid clearly *identifying* the problem. You can help your students avoid this tendency by having them take a long look at the problems they want to ameliorate.

You should also weave problem-solving skills and perspectives into what you do in your courses because all human beings like to solve problems. It leads to happiness and a feeling of power. Failure to improve conditions leads to the opposite.

What: Conduct problem-solving exercises. It is good to use exercises like these early in the course, but they can be used anywhere in your course and for any content purpose. The first step of the exercise is to identify a problem that students face that means something to them. You should not allow them to identify a policy they don't like, such as high tuition, as a "problem." Instead, it could be something like "too much student debt."

Once they have identified a problem, they should complete the following steps and prepare a brief memo or presentation:

1. State the problem clearly.
2. Provide evidence of the existence of the problem.
3. List the factors contributing to the problem.
4. Suggest a policy to ameliorate the problem and indicate why this policy might work.
5. Indicate the likelihood that those in power will adopt the policy.

These five steps are a basic requirement of any problem-solving process. You may want to revise the steps as you see fit for your content area. This can be done as an individual assignment or, preferably, as a team activity, and it's especially useful for students working to improve their own campus. Not only does this help them develop useful skills, it also provides you with an understanding of what your students see happening on campus.

Materials Needed: Directions listing the five steps of the problem-solving process

Where: The classroom

Skill Sets Practiced: Solving Problems; Asking and Answering the Right Questions; Working Directly with People

Chapter Thirty-Six

The Order, Freedom, Equality Triangle

Three Is a Magic Number

—*Schoolhouse Rock!*

A good way to help students think about big societal problems that lead to policy debates is to look at society in terms of the three concepts of order, freedom, equality (see figures 36.1–2).

These three concepts can be applied to all kinds of decisions, ranging from parents and their teenage children deciding whether there should be a curfew to the president of the United States and members of Congress deciding on tax rates for citizens. The three concepts are values relating to any given decision, and one of these values will be more important to any given individual. And you might remind your students that tension over priorities is a constant in life.

Even though there is always disagreement over which value is most important, everyone would agree that order, freedom, and equality must be in some kind of equilibrium. Order may be viewed as more important than freedom or equality if, say, your house is invaded, but there are always limits.

The use of these values as a framework to discuss today's society is an extension of the continuums discussed in chapter 34. The triangle of order, freedom, and equality implies three continuums: order-freedom; order-equality; and freedom-equality, each of which limits the other.

Professors have long tried to help students understand societal tradeoffs and their resulting tensions, which can have a major impact on society. In a political science course, a professor will have the student read John Locke, Thomas Hobbes, and other writers on democracy and conditions in society. The triangle framework suggested here is just another way to discuss democ-

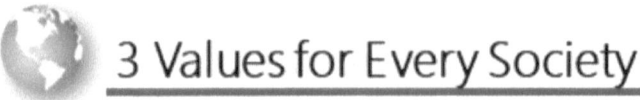

3 Values for Every Society

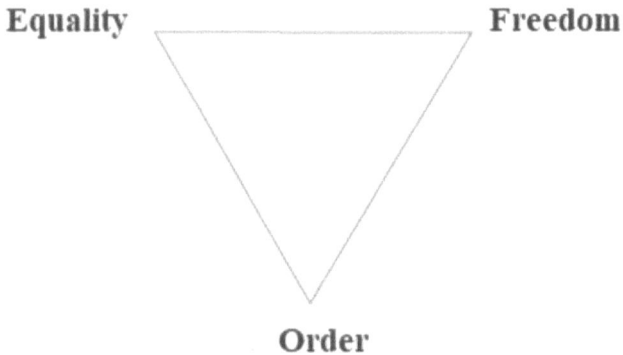

Figure 36.1.

racy and current political controversies without requiring reading historical materials. For example, Locke tended to argue that freedom was more important than order while Hobbes took the opposite position.

There is no evidence that studying traditional political theories leads to changes in the behavior of citizens. The life of the mind is not the same thing as life. Moreover, these political theory discussions are housed in the disciplines of political science and philosophy, which the majority of undergraduates don't even take.

To be fair, there is also no evidence that the approaches suggested work. All tactics in education are a matter of the experiences of the professor. They require that you test them to see if they work for you.

Citizenship requires that we think about society as a whole and in a framework that makes room for the tensions among order, freedom, and equality. No matter what field you teach, you may want to have your students look at the societal impact of whatever you are teaching in terms of the tradeoffs of order, freedom, and equality.

What: Show figures 36.1–2 and then have a general discussion with the entire class in less than 10 minutes. Give an example of how some societal conditions and policies show the conflict between order, freedom, and equality.

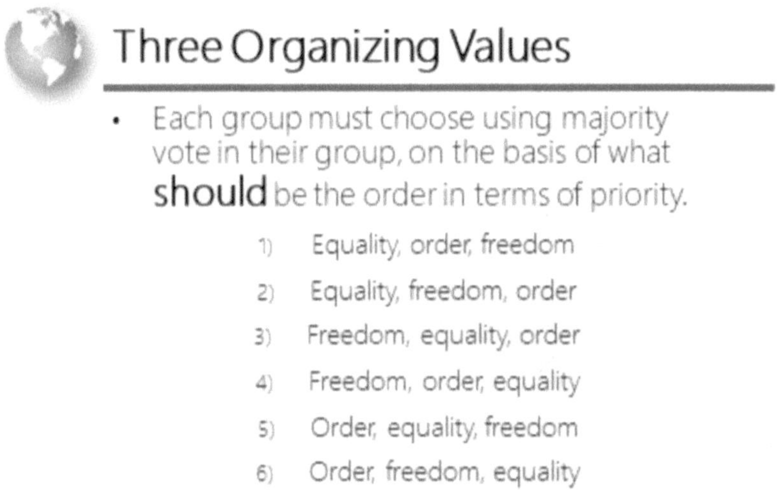

Three Organizing Values

- Each group must choose using majority vote in their group, on the basis of what **should** be the order in terms of priority.
    1) Equality, order, freedom
    2) Equality, freedom, order
    3) Freedom, equality, order
    4) Freedom, order, equality
    5) Order, equality, freedom
    6) Order, freedom, equality

Figure 36.2.

After this, break the class into groups of three or more depending on the size of the class. Leave up figure 36.2 and tell the groups to make a decision on which priority among the six choices they like. Give them 5 to 15 minutes. Then ask a member of each group to stand and state the number chosen by the majority of the group. After all the groups have responded and you have listed the number of those who supported each given choice, conduct an open discussion.

This exercise will get students to think about their views of the ideal balance between order, freedom, and equality. In thinking about themselves, they can think about the tradeoffs in their personal lives between their needs and the three values. They should also see the tensions inherent here and develop preferences on what the balance should be among the three for how they see things as they now are and for how they would like them to be.

Materials Needed: Figures 36.1 and 36.2 of this chapter
Where: The classroom
Skill Sets Practiced: Communicating Verbally; Working Directly with People; Influencing People; Asking and Answering the Right Questions; Solving Problems

Chapter Thirty-Seven

The Grading Exercise

> One learns through the heart, not the eyes or the intellect.
>
> —Mark Twain

About 20 years ago, a philosophy professor who was displeased with his students' participation in class and coursework announced one day that he would give all students in his class an A if they voted for him to do so. To his surprise, one student objected, and then the class voted not to accept his offer. The discussion led to a more engaged class for the rest of the semester.

This led to the development of the grading exercise described below. It should be conducted halfway into the course, when the students have a stake. The most important dynamic here is that you promise to make a change if there is a clear vote. In effect, you will be giving them limited power over your authority, but it is worth the risk. This is not a simulation or a game but a reality for the students since their grade in the course is at stake.

The students will expend a lot of energy trying to come to a decision in the exercise. That energy will lead to more student engagement throughout the remainder of the course. The students will learn that conflicting interests can lead to gridlock and that voting procedures are almost as important as the substance of the decision.

Running this exercise in class provides you not only with entertainment but also with a way to identify leaders. It also gives you a way to provide advice on the importance of choosing strategies and following the advice in Dale Carnegie's book *How to Win Friends and Influence People*. Additionally, it gives you insight into the attitudes of the students on the conflict between self-interest and the public interest. Unfortunately, self-interest dominates despite some genuflecting toward the public interest. You will also see their attitudes toward meritocracy and equality. But this exercise is not just about politics. It is about good citizenship, and it could be used in any field as either a simulation or an exercise with binding consequences.

What: The class selects one of three predetermined policies aimed at the problem that "students do not learn as much as they should from this excellent book and course." Three grading policies will be considered remedies for this problem. For the purposes of this exercise, it is assumed that all class members agree on their need to increase their level of learning in the course (see appendix A for complete student instructions).

After a period of class discussion, the class should decide which of the following three grading systems you, the professor, will use:

1. The traditional system, which is the system most professors use and in which letter grades are allocated in the following way:

Grade	Numerical Score
A	93–100
A-	90–92
B+	87–89
B	83–86
B-	80–82
C+	77–79
C	73–76
C-	70–72
D	60–69
F	Below 60

2. A conservative system in which students who receive the top 35% of the scores are guaranteed at least an A-; the next 15% receive at least a B; the next 35% receive at least a C-; the next 10% receive a D; and the remaining 5% receive an F.
3. A socialist system in which students are guaranteed at least an A- if they are in the top 10% while the next 60% receive at least a B-; the next 15% are guaranteed at least a C-; the next 10% receive a D; and the remaining 5% receive an F if their scores are below those of the traditional system.

If either a conservative or socialist system is chosen, students who would be better off with the traditional system will receive the grade designated under the traditional system. The conservative and socialist systems are subsidies and cannot be used to penalize students who would be better off under the traditional system. In other words, these systems are designed to raise grades, and they will not cause anyone to receive a lower grade.

After discussion of these three grading systems, have your students make a decision according to the following rules:

1. The final policy must be one of the three systems.
2. If the class fails to reach a decision by the end of the exercise, the traditional system will stay in effect.
3. The instructor will chair the class meeting.
4. The class can reach a decision in one of two ways: by unanimous agreement of everyone in the class, or, if no unanimous agreement can be reached, by use of a voting procedure such as two-thirds majority, simple majority, or any other procedure. However, there must be unanimous agreement on the voting procedure.
5. Unruly behavior will result in one minute of silence.

Materials Needed: The complete student exercise instructions given in appendix A. Feel free to change the instructions as you see fit.

Where: The classroom

Skill Sets Practiced: Taking Responsibility; Communicating Verbally; Working Directly with People; Influencing People; Asking and Answering the Right Questions; Solving Problems

Chapter Thirty-Eight

The Prince System

> There is nothing more difficult to carry out, nor more doubtful of success, nor more dangerous to handle, than to initiate a new order of things.
> —Niccolo Machiavelli

Today's students are long on idealism and short on realism. Although professors can expect this given the naiveté of youth and the idealism embedded in our culture and education system, a balance is clearly needed for adulthood. College-age students tend to not be able to balance their desire for a better world with the reality of whether or not those in power will accept change. Those trying to make change as opposed to discussing change know this struggle all too well.

Reading case studies and listening to lectures on how good ideas do or do not get implemented at any level is a good start. Students also need a rigorous framework to use when thinking about support for and opposition to their ideas, whether it is convincing their parents to buy them a car, getting a stop sign put up on their street, getting a sorority or fraternity to raise funds for a charity, or changing government policies.

The Prince System was developed by one of the author's colleagues, Michael K. O'Leary, alongside the professor in the early 1970s. It helped develop a political-risk forecasting system for business, and they used it to demonstrate to the U.S. Department of State and the Central Intelligence Agency how to make political forecasts.

The system is based on the commonsense idea that if you add all the positive and one-half the neutral forces in a system for a given decision and divide by the absolute sum, you will get a probability that forecasts the decision. This is an idea every experienced politician, boss, or leader instinctively knows. They may not use the system explicitly by filling out a Prince

Chart, but they use the system by reflex as a result of the experience and mentoring they have received.

For the inexperienced, the system gives them a process to make a forecast. The accuracy of the forecast depends on the knowledge of the person using it. It therefore requires students to do research to predict the likelihood of the success of their idea. That research alone will help turn students from idealists who think a good idea will be inevitably adopted to serious and competent citizens who can create and adapt ideas that will work.

Since the Prince System is designed to help forecast any given decision, you may find it useful in your own professional life. It can be applied to tenure and promotion, getting a raise, getting acceptance for a new course, or any decision that needs agreement among two or more people. Using the system will help you avoid two extremes: believing a good idea will be accepted because it is a good idea, and believing your idea has no chance of being implemented because people don't like change or you. In the case of too much negativity, it may help you find the players who are blocking the decision you want and figure out how modifying your idea might increase its chances of approval.

Many of you may already have the Prince System embedded in your thinking even though you do not use physical Prince Charts. If so, you must be more successful than others who don't. If you use the system for your own decision-making, you will be more effective in getting your students to do the same.

What: A brief description on how to use the Prince System appears in appendix B. After your students read it, do a Prince Chart in class on some policy desired at your college such as "Maintain the current level of tuition." This will introduce your students to the Prince System. You may then want them to make a chart on a policy they support. You can have the students do this in groups or individually. It is best to first ask the students how likely they think the decision they want to happen will happen and then ask them to contrast their prediction with the forecast that the system produces. Usually they are hopelessly naive and generate a 90% likelihood, but when they do a Prince Chart, they will usually produce a Prince Chart–based forecast under 40%.

Materials Needed: Appendix B and a Prince Chart
Where: The classroom
Skill Sets Practiced: Influencing People; Solving Problems; Asking and Answering the Right Questions

Conclusion

Where Do You Go From Here?

> Man is born free; and everywhere he is in chains.
> —Jean Jacques Rousseau, *The Social Contract*

You have surely figured out by now that this book is not just a self-help guide for professors in all fields who want to do a little better and be a lot happier. It is also a call for a revolution in undergraduate education. If the roles, strategies, and tactics introduced here were practiced widely, it would lead to a transformation to adjust to the broad social and economic changes in higher education required by the GI Bill. Although the GI Bill was created more than 70 years ago, higher-education faculty have yet to adjust to the career and citizenship goals required by the principle of college for all. The transformation entailed would recognize the importance of the individuality of the learner, of skills for careers and citizenship, and of experiential learning.

While accepting the advice in this book will improve your happiness as a professor, you don't have to be a revolutionary. The tactics and practices are for your benefit, regardless of your stance on what undergraduate education should be. The trade-off between skills and content as well as between the trinity of reading, lectures, and experiential learning is up to you.

The current state of undergraduate education is shifting, but very slowly. Following the suggestions in this book will place you in the middle of the shift. You will recognize benefits of an education that gives students more opportunities to develop their citizenship and career potential without trying to topple the old regime. If you teach in a liberal arts or general education framework and you adopt these suggestions, you will not be circling the wagons or be calling for the end of the humanities. You will be pragmatically adjusting what you do by keeping your students' and society's needs in mind.

The goals of this book will be accomplished if you test a few of the ideas suggested in it in your own classroom. The suggestions will help you reduce your anger and frustration over your inability to have most of your students learn the content of your discipline. You will have accepted that the right thing to do, in addition to meeting your traditional educational goals, is to satisfy the needs of all undergraduates from all ethnic groups and socioeconomic levels as they prepare for a career and citizenship.

Fighting for or against a massive revolution is not the way to happiness. Having fun with your students is. When you have helped students find careers they like and become responsible citizens, they and their parents will get what they have been promised. The government and society will benefit too. The happiest shopkeepers are those who have customers who feel they get what they pay for. Happy customers produce happy shopkeepers.

You are honoring the implicit social contract that has given you the opportunity to be an undergraduate professor. The more you honor that contract, the happier you will be.

Appendix A

The Grading Exercise: Student Guide and Discussion Following the Exercise

This appendix provides the full grading exercise plus some ideas you may want to use in introducing and debriefing the exercise. Students will be emotional in their discussion, so this gives you the opportunity to emphasize the need for reason in making decisions. This appendix consists of two sections. The Student Guide should be shared with the students. The Discussion Following the Exercise can be given to the students or you can use it to help you guide the discussion.

STUDENT GUIDE

This guide can be reproduced for class use.

One type of policy by which you as a student are greatly affected is the grading policy operating in your class. The way in which the instructor assigns grades impacts the grade you receive for the course. While instructors have the power to make this decision, they can also allow you and the rest of your classmates to take part in the decision. This transforms you from a stakeholder to a player. In this exercise, you will not only gain experience in the making of a policy that affects you, you will explore the role that public- and private-interest goals play in shaping your behavior and the behavior of your class. This exercise gives you the opportunity to select how letter grades will be assigned to the numerical score you achieve on assignments and tests for this class.

In this exercise, you as a class will select one of three policies aimed at the problem that "students do not learn as much as they should from this excellent book and course." Three grading policies will be considered remedies for this problem. For the purposes of this exercise, it is assumed that all class members agree on their need to increase their level of learning in this course.

This exercise assumes that your teacher now marks according to the traditional system in which letter grades are allocated in the following way:

Grade	Numerical Score
A	93–100
A-	90–92
B+	87–89
B	83–86
B-	80–82
C+	77–79
C	73–76
C-	70–72
D	60–69
F	Below 60

After a period of class discussion, you will reach a decision as to which of the following three grading systems your class will use:

1. The traditional system described above.
2. A conservative system in which the students who receive the top 35% of the scores are guaranteed at least an A- while the next 15% receive at least a B; the next 35% receive at least a C-; the next 10% receive a D; and the remaining 5% receive an F.
3. A socialist system in which the students who receive the top 10% of the scores are guaranteed at least an A- while the next 60% receive at least a B-; the next 15% are guaranteed at least a C-; the next 10% receive a D; and the remaining 5% receive an F if their scores are below those for the traditional system.

If either a conservative or socialist system is chosen, students who would be better off with the traditional system will receive the grade designated under the traditional system. The conservative and socialist systems are subsidies to benefit different types of students. They cannot be used to penalize students who would be better off under the traditional system. In other words, these systems are designed to raise grades, and they will not cause anyone to receive a lower grade.

By participating in this exercise, you will learn about the way in which what is perceived to be best for the individual (an increased chance of higher grades) can conflict with what is perceived as best for the class as a whole (maximum learning for everyone). This conflict between self-interest and public interest is at the heart of all policy decisions. In addition, you will gain insight into other conditions surrounding the making of public policy such as the conflict between minority and majority rights, respect for others, obstacles to a responsible and representative decision, freedom of choice, leadership, and equitable rewards for talent and hard work.

As a class, you will make a decision according to the following rules:

1. The final policy must be one of the three systems.
2. If the class fails to reach a decision by the end of the exercise, the traditional system will stay in effect.
3. The instructor will chair the class meeting.
4. The class can reach a decision in one of two ways: by unanimous agreement of everyone in the class, or, if no unanimous agreement can be reached, by use of a voting procedure such as two-thirds majority, simple majority, or any other procedure. However, there must be unanimous agreement on the voting procedure.
5. Unruly behavior will result in one minute of silence.

DISCUSSION FOLLOWING THE EXERCISE

Once you have participated in the grading exercise, you should be able to explore the kinds of goals that motivated you, your classmates, and your instructor.

Possible public-interest goals include the following:

1. Promoting more learning
2. Promoting equality
3. Creating a more just system
4. Maintaining order
5. Protecting majority rights
6. Protecting minority rights

Possible private-interest goals for the members of the class include the following:

1. Less stress

2. Less work
3. Higher grades

The kinds of goals and questions raised by this grading exercise can be found in every organization from your family to the United Nations. All public policies benefit different segments of society and create difficulties for others, just as the traditional system would result in lower grades for the less-hardworking members of the class than would the socialist system. The conflict between majority and minority rights developed in this exercise is similar to the conflict between the majority and minority over voting rights and equality of opportunity in the United States. To the extent that the conservative and socialist systems are systems that provide subsidies to different groups, they raise questions similar to those raised about subsidies to farmers, tax credits to businesses, and tariffs on imports.

Disagreement among players in this grading exercise can also occur over means. Both sides may accept increased learning as a major goal, but those calling for a socialist system might argue that by reducing stress over grades, more learning would be achieved, while those calling for the traditional system would say that competition produces more learning.

You should also recognize in your behavior and the behavior of others the relative strength of public and private interests. You may be looking for a higher grade for yourself but are putting your arguments in public interest terms (e.g., you claim that the class will learn more), while traditionalists who argue that they are only trying to preserve order might be accused of trying to enjoy more personal satisfaction by raising the level of competition in the class.

In a similar way, a variety of analogies may be developed relating to past and current real-world public policy issues. Look for the similarities and realize that the policies of local, state, and federal governments will have a direct impact on goals important to you personally and to the society in which you live.

Appendix B

Directions for Forecasting with the Prince System

The Prince System is a method for forecasting the chances that a decision will be made where more than one individual or group has significant influence. To simplify the discussion, I will use the word "decision" for the remainder of this guide but it can mean a policy, a program, or a specific act.

The Prince System requires the following steps to make a forecast:

Step 1: Identify the decision to be made.
Step 2: Identify the players likely to have a direct or indirect impact on the decision.
Step 3: Determine issue position: whether each player supports, opposes, or is neutral toward the decision. Determine power: how effective each player would be in blocking the decision, helping to make it happen, or otherwise affecting the implementation of the decision. Determine priority: how important the decision is to each player.
Step 4: Calculate the likelihood that the decision will be implemented.

Each of these steps to make forecasts of decisions is described below. The information that you use applies only on the day you complete the four steps. The Prince Chart and its forecast presents a static picture of the decision, players, positions, and likelihood at the time the chart is completed. Changes in the real world occur frequently, and they can change your forecast. But you have to start somewhere; just be ready to change the numbers if conditions change.

STEP 1: IDENTIFY THE DECISION TO BE MADE

Begin by clearly describing the decision. This decision can be undertaken by any organization—government, nonprofit, business—and also at any level of the organization.

Be sure that you have defined a decision and not a goal. For example, "Reducing unemployment" is a goal; "Spending $10 million of federal funds to provide job-training programs" is a decision.

Although the decision needs to be clearly described in order to forecast its implementation, the exact details of its final formulation are not required. Frequently, proposed decisions are altered to gain the support needed for their approval. For instance, you may want a 10% increase in your budget and then eventually reduce the proposal to 5% if you think 10% will not be supported.

The following hypothetical case study provides the description of a decision to deal with the problem of drug abuse in the community of Riverdale.

The Riverdale Youth Bureau wants to create a court with teenagers as judges to try and sentence youths eighteen and under who are accused of buying, selling, or using drugs.

This Teen Court would sentence the offenders to rehabilitation, community service, or serving time on the Teen Court. This program will be controlled by the County Youth Bureau.

New legislation is not needed for implementation of the policy, and all administrative duties will be performed by the program director.

The court will be administered by a new staff person whose salary, expenses, and administrative costs will total $56,000.

No formal court action is required, but the district attorney and the town justice will have to agree to allow this court to operate informally.

STEP 2: IDENTIFY THE PLAYERS

Players are any individuals or organizations who have some influence over the decision. They may have official authority to make the decision or have some significant influence over those who do have the authority.

Identifying players is one of the most important steps in the Prince System. Including unimportant players or omitting important players can distort the analysis to the extent that it becomes useless. A key to identifying the correct players is to consider the legislative, administrative, and judicial requirements of the decision. If the decision will involve monetary concerns, include players that have authority over the budget. If the decision will involve new or revised legislation, include the chief executive and the legislature. If the decision will involve neither new funds nor new legislation, include the bureaucracies responsible for the decision and also include those that influence those bureaucracies. In addition to government officials in the executive and legislative branch, include players representing key interest groups.

To develop your list of players, begin by writing down all those that you think will have some degree of influence on the decision. Next, reduce the list depending on how much time and interest you have. As few as 5 players can be used to make a quick and dirty forecast. For a more accurate forecast, 50 or even 100 players could be used if you have a lot of time and money. Generally, 10 players makes sense.

To limit the number of players, group individuals and organizations into collective players for the purpose of analysis. The process of grouping frequently appears arbitrary and can seriously affect the results if it is not done carefully. Guidelines to use in grouping players to improve the accuracy of the analysis include the following:

- Group players having the same economic interests. In dealing with an environmental issue, for example, all private developers could be grouped together.
- Do not group players with veto power. This especially holds for governmental players. For example, for federal decisions, never group the president and Congress.
- Do not group players if there is a disagreement among them or if their components have widely unequal power. For example, members of a city government could be combined as a single player if there is general agreement among them concerning the issue and if each person in the governing unit has approximately equal power. If there are disagreements or if some members are much more powerful than others, it is preferable to divide them into two (or more) players.

Select a list of players that represents a reasonable picture of the overall power distribution. Do not include an excess of players that give one side unrealistic weight. If there is one collective player with an immense amount of power, that player should be divided into enough smaller players so that the total power is accurately reflected. For example, in dealing with the legislative branch, you might want to list the House of Representatives and the Senate as separate players rather than treating Congress as a single player.

These guidelines are intentionally general. Your judgment in conducting the analysis is vital at every step, and the selection of players will have a major impact on your forecast. Your success depends on becoming knowledgeable enough to select the right group of players.

Here are the players selected for the proposed Riverdale Teen Court decision:

- James French, district attorney of Riverdale. His consent, with that of the town justice, is necessary to create the court.
- Johanna Horton, town justice. Her consent, along with that of French, is necessary to create the court.
- Joyce Zeno, County Youth Bureau. She is responsible for approving youth-related programs in the county.
- K. Westcott, deputy director for Local Services in the Division for Youth. She has the authority to allocate funds for youth programs in the state.
- J. McGrath, chief of the Riverdale Police. McGraf would have to cooperate with French and Horton for the program to operate effectively.

STEP 3: ESTIMATE THE ISSUE POSITION, POWER, AND PRIORITIES OF EACH PLAYER

For each player, you will need to estimate the three attributes of issue position, power, and priority. The number you assign must be based on a solid knowledge of the players.

Issue position is the current attitude of the player toward the decision. It is expressed as a number ranging from +5 to -5 to indicate levels of support or opposition. Assign +5 if the player is firmly in favor of the issue and is unlikely to change. A +4, +3, +2, or +1 indicates lower levels of firmness of the player's support, while a neutral position is expressed as 0. Similarly, a -5 indicates firm opposition, and a -4, -3, -2, or -1 indicates lower degrees of opposition. When estimating a player's issue position,

- read and listen to what the player says about the issue;
- estimate from the player's economic, social, or political standing what the player's position is likely to be on the basis of self-interest; and
- look for differences among individuals and factions within groups and organizations. Look for inconsistencies in statements by individual members. If the contrasting positions seem evenly balanced, assign a 0 (neutral) issue position. If there seems a very small positive or negative balance toward the issue, assign a +1 or -1 for the player's issue position.

Power is defined as the degree to which one player, relative to the other players, can directly or indirectly exert influence concerning the decision. A player's power is based on such factors as group size, wealth, physical resources, institutional authority, prestige, and political skill. Power is expressed as a number ranging from 1 to 5. Assign 1 if the player has a slight amount of power; 2 if the player has more than minimum power; 3 or 4 if the player has substantial power; or 5 if the player can veto or prevent the implementation of the policy with little or no interference by other players. When estimating a player's power,

- ask yourself if the player has the ability either to block or to implement the decision;
- determine if legal authority is a consideration;
- consider whether the player has the ability to help or hinder the decision-making process;
- determine, if need be, the player's wealth;
- do not assume that a player, powerful on one set of issues, is necessarily powerful on all issues; and
- consider the allies and enemies of the player. Powerful allies increase power; powerful enemies diminish it.

Priority is defined as the importance that the player attaches to supporting or opposing the decision relative to all other decisions the player has to make. Priority is expressed as a number ranging from 1 to 5. Assign 1 to indicate a slight interest or concern for the issue, regardless of the player's issue position and power. Assign 2 for those players with some concern, and assign 3 or 4 to indicate substantial concern. A 5 is reserved for those players that give their highest priority to the issue. When estimating priority,

- determine the frequency and intensity with which the player makes public statements about the issue;
- from the player's social, political, and economic interest, determine the importance the player is likely to attach to the decision;
- watch out for the fact that priority can be rapidly and substantially altered by external events and the intrusion of other issues; and
- remember that other issues and factors compete for the player's attention and, hence, priority.

STEP 4: COMPLETE A PRINCE CHART AND CALCULATE THE LIKELY OUTCOME

After making estimates of issue position, power, and priority for each player, you can determine the probable outcome of the decision. See tables B.1–2 for a Prince Chart that applies to our Riverdale Teen Court example and Prince Chart steps and calculation rules.

Table B.1. Prince Chart

POLICY: Implement a Teen Court in Riverdale

(State in terms of desired political outcome)

PLAYERS	ISSUE POSITION	x	POWER	x	PRIORITY	=	PRINCE SCORE
James French	+1	x	5	x	1	=	+5
Johanna Horton	0	x	5	x	3	=	(15)
Joyce Zeno	+4	x	5	x	3	=	+60
K. Westcott	-2	x	5	x	1	=	-10
J. McGrath	-4	x	3	x	3	=	-36

Table B.2. Prince Chart Calculations

Step 1: Players	Step 2: Position (+5 to -5)	x	Step 3: Power (1 to 5)	x	Step 4: Priority	=	Step 5: Prince Score

About the Author

Bill Coplin received his BA in social science from Johns Hopkins University in 1960 and his MA (1962) and PhD (1964) in international relations from American University. He has been director and a professor of the Policy Studies Program of the Maxwell School of Syracuse University and College of Arts and Sciences since 1976. He has published more than 116 books and articles in the fields of international relations, public policy, political risk analysis, education, and citizenship, and he has won most of the teaching and advising awards offered by Syracuse University.

www.ingramcontent.com/pod-product-compliance
Lightning Source LLC
Chambersburg PA
CBHW020747230426
43665CB00009B/530